MW01631129

Reflections from Encouraged Moms

"Before I had my baby, I knew I wanted to breastfeed but wasn't sure if I could. Gloria encouraged me to commit to just two weeks and go from there. Starting was difficult, but Gloria understood how moms need emotional support first and breastfeeding advice second. We got past two weeks and just kept going and going, tackling each stage of the process as it arrived. Gloria's heart for breastfeeding is evident in her heart for mothers."

-Holly and Sophie

"There are so many moving pieces with breastfeeding. I was absolutely determined to feed my son to the very best of my capacity after having a breast reduction some years ago. There are some good books out there, but getting Gloria Dudney to help me from the beginning has made the difference between success and frustration – perhaps even failure from inexperience. To have attained this level of success and normalcy is a prayer answered and pretty rare for our circumstances. Having Gloria's expertise has not only made breastfeeding after a reduction possible, but my baby and I have enjoyed the best possible outcome! I am so grateful for her and her calling to help mothers and babies."

-Ashley and Silvan

"As a new mother, I knew I wanted to breastfeed my child from the beginning. But once I was faced with the task, it was truly a struggle. I never realized all that went into breastfeeding because it seemed like an easy, natural thing to do, but man was I wrong. I hit road block after road block pretty much every week. I cried a lot, wanted to give up many times, but then felt guilty. With the help of Gloria, my lactation consultant, and doing endless research, I was able to tackle each road block one day at a time. Thankfully by the 3rd month, things slowly started to fall into place. Even though I pump half the time since I work full-time, it's still rewarding. Never giving up and having a resource to turn to has kept me going."

-Laura and Justin

"Gloria is a fighter for this incredible gift of nursing. I needed her, and she was there when I was at the weakest I have ever been physically and yet had a responsibility to love my baby and give him the best thing for him! Full of sound advice and encouragement, her approach MATTERS, and I pray she never gives up!"

-Neva and Micah

"The thing I appreciate most about Gloria is her support after I discontinued nursing. That helped so much, especially since I had some guilt issues with it all. My husband and I are loving parenthood, enjoying every day!"

-Nikki and Kendall

"With Gloria's kindness and help, I breastfed my first baby for 13 months. My second baby was very different. We needed complex and sustained lactation support due to his very slow growth, tongue tie, and other challenges. I was about to throw in the towel when he still was not growing normally at 4 months old, and multiple gastrointestinal specialists advised me to immediately wean to formula. I was heartbroken, but of course I complied with their advice. However, my mother's intuition told me that my milk was not the problem. Gloria encouraged me to trust my instincts and suggested I exclusively pump and store my milk for a month just in case he didn't grow well on formula. And he didn't. It was eventually discovered that he has a rare genetic disorder that was the cause of his failure to thrive. He had a feeding tube placed for additional nutrition and, now at nearly a year of age, he continues to receive the countless benefits of breast milk. When I despaired that all options were exhausted, Gloria provided one last option. She helped me so that I could help him."

-Mallorie, Londyn, and Nolan

"Even though I knew I would not rest well for a while with a new baby, I rested a lot easier knowing that Gloria's approach to breastfeeding had greatly helped us with our first baby and would do so again."

-Melissa, Madison, and Mackenzie

"The first 3 weeks of my daughter's life were some of the hardest of mine. I never imagined how challenging breastfeeding could be, but Gloria's consistent hopefulness, patience, and encouragement made it possible. By the end of those 3 weeks, Gloria had helped me exhaust every resource to increase my milk supply. Nothing seemed to work, but by the grace of God and Gloria's persistence with telling me that I could do it (and assurance that even if I didn't, I was still a good mom), I have been able to breastfeed Clara Grace ever since. I truly consider it a miracle and am grateful every time I am able to nurse her."

-Lindsey and Clara Grace

"Because of the absolutely terrible and traumatic experience I had attempting to breastfeed my son, I was determined that I wouldn't even try with my daughter. But she latched on like a champ at birth and, with Gloria's advice and encouragement in her first 2 weeks, we kept going – and kept going! She is 8 months old now and we're going to go as long as we can!"

-Sarah and Keira

"Gloria encouraged me to stick with breastfeeding while being totally supportive of my needs. Being a mom is more than feeding. Gloria never made me feel pressured. She just adapted her knowledgeable and caring support to my ever-changing mind."

-Sara, Luke, and Nate

"Becoming a mother has been the most rewarding, yet challenging, thing I have ever done. I thought because I was a nurse, I had some knowledge of what to expect with my first breastfeeding – boy, was I wrong! I had it pictured as a beautiful, intimate bonding experience with my son. I never imagined I would face all the difficulties I did. Gloria helped me accept our reality and offered hope when it felt like there was none."

-Whitney and Leland

"It was always my dream to breastfeed, but little did I know that I would be up against all sorts of challenges: inverted nipples, lip and tongue tie, an oversupply for a short time. I thought I would never be free from that breast pump...But I am! Gloria guided me every step of the way and kept me grounded when I truly felt like giving up. Now my beautiful 4-month old can latch all on her own and feed efficiently, and I am pain free! We did it!"

-Courtney and Harper

Mommy-Friendly Breastfeeding

Logical Solutions for Challenges

and

Encouragement for Enjoying Your Baby

A Daily Guide

FIRST EDITION

Gloria Dudney, RN, BSN, IBCLC, RLC

Mommy-Friendly Breastfeeding

Gloria Dudney, RN, BSN, IBCLC, RLC

ISBN- 978-0-99993577-1-2 (paperback)

Published by Mommy-Friendly Breastfeeding

Johnson City, Tennessee

Photos used by permission from

Lisa Smith of LHS Photography, Cover photo and pages 114, 115

Medela, Inc., pages 33, 35

Sara Reed, IBCLC, pages 14, 16-19, 22

Carrie Stiles Miller, pages 27, 33, 35, 59

Cover design and pages 87-91 by Sara Reed, IBCLC

Printed in the United States of America

To LaVada Fife,

the original mommy-friendly nurse

Smarter than she knew, stronger than we knew

Contents

Part 1

Breastfeeding Rescue

Breastfeeding Rescue

Be encouraged!

No matter what, everything is going to be ok. The endless advice you're receiving from various healthcare providers, family, friends, Facebook, Twitter, Instagram, Snapchat, and a vast assortment of websites can make you doubt yourself. You start to believe that everything is *not* going to be ok and that you're never going to measure up to all of these expectations. **Don't let the information age steal your joy.** Your journey is going to look different than the journeys of even your closest friends and family. You are an individual, and you will need individualized care. This book will provide a guide for navigating your journey with flexible tools designed to help you achieve your goals, ***as defined by you***.

If you are an expecting mom, welcome to the next chapter in your life. You are bringing a new life into the world. And, especially when it your first baby, it will probably be the most wonderful, and at the same time terrifying, experience of your life. Be patient with yourself, don't panic if you encounter difficulty you had not anticipated, keep your sense of humor, and trust your instincts. Above all, enjoy your baby! Becoming familiar with the topics covered in this book will prepare you for conquering the challenges most common to early infant feeding and sleeping behaviors.

If you are already a breastfeeding mom and are not experiencing any pain or problems, that is wonderful news! You will find portions of this book helpful, particularly the **Days and Nights Mixed Up** care plan on page 28 and updated information regarding pacifiers on page 45, among other things. If you would like to track your progress, you can use the **Combination Milk Journals** starting on page 98 and disregard any area that doesn't apply to you.

If you a breastfeeding mom and are experiencing pain and other problems, we're going to conquer those challenges together. If it isn't going the way you pictured yet, don't despair. Breastfeeding a newborn can be really difficult. It gets easier. In the meantime, this text will offer you **logical solutions** that are designed to protect your long-term goals. Be encouraged that you're not doing it wrong. You're not failing at anything. You may just need some options and a little rest. Try not to become overwhelmed by looking too far into the future. Don't worry about making it 6 months; just focus on making it 6 days.

If you feel like you are battling your own body or battling your own baby, that can feel like a lose-lose situation. If you are receiving conflicting information from every medical professional who advises you, that can feel intensely frustrating and maybe even a little frightening because you're not sure who to believe. What might help the most is to simply **trust your own instincts and focus on the two main goals of early breastfeeding: soft breasts and a happy baby**. In other words, if your baby is relaxed after feedings and peeing and pooping as he should for his day of age, he is basically "happy". And if milk is being removed from your breasts regularly, which helps prevent infection and protects your milk supply, your breasts are basically drained and "soft". The rest is just details. Very specific guidance on how to achieve those two main goals is detailed in this book.

If you experiencing significant difficulty, it's ok if you need to pump your milk into bottles for your baby right now. As long as you're protecting your milk supply, you are protecting your breastfeeding future. You have options that you may have thought you didn't have. Check out the **Combination Feeding Option** on page 36 and be encouraged!

Let's get started!

Using This Book

Challenges Flowchart

On pages 8 and 9, a flowchart asks "What is Your Breastfeeding Challenge?" That flowchart directs you to some solutions for specific challenges. For example, if it hurts to breastfeed, you will find page numbers for the care plans specific to address nipple and breast pain. If you are having trouble keeping your baby awake to feed well during the day but he seems to be very alert at night, you will find the page number for the care plan that offers solutions for his days and nights being mixed up.

Care Plans

On pages 11 through 60, the specific plans of care for many common breastfeeding challenges are found. The **Breastfeeding Challenge Flowchart** and **Table of Contents** provide a quick guide to the page numbers.

Making Sense of it All

On pages 63-68, the **Challenges** section reviews why your unique prenatal and birth reality requires a unique approach to your breastfeeding reality. On pages 69 through 83, you will find a detailed description of the **Priorities** to keep in mind as you achieve your breastfeeding goals. Knowing that your long-term breastfeeding relationship is being protected, you can more calmly work through the process of feeding your baby and protecting your milk supply.

Appendix

On pages 85-96, miscellaneous helpful references are gathered for you to use as needed.

Milk Journals

On pages 97-129, daily journals designed to help you track your and your baby's progress are provided. There are two sets of journals. The **Combination Journals** are for moms who are doing a combination of nursing directly from the breast **and** bottle feedings of expressed breast milk and/or formula. The **Exclusively Pumping Journals** are for moms who are expressing their breast milk for their babies instead of nursing their babies directly from the breast. You may find that you will go back and forth between the sets as your situation changes. The journals are numbered for days 1-14 of age, but if your baby is beyond that age, you can use the day 14 journal and copy it as many times as needed.

What this book is not

Not a replacement for medical care. Consult your obstetrician, pediatrician, and/or lactation consultant with any breastfeeding difficulties you are experiencing.

Not an exhaustive breastfeeding reference book. There are several breastfeeding books that cover all the bases (*Breastfeeding Made Simple* by Mohrbacher and Kendall-Tackett is an excellent, succinct guide). The goal of this text is to provide what you must know quickly in a crisis to protect your long-term breastfeeding goals. The text repeatedly encourages you to follow up in person with an IBCLC.

Not necessarily in agreement with everything you have read and been told about how to achieve breastfeeding "success". What "should" be happening is often not what "is" happening. This does not make you a failure. In life, there is typically more than one way to do things. You're a great mom and success is defined by you. You may just need some real-world feeding options. This text is full of options and was developed over the course of 25 years caring for and brain-storming with moms, dads, and babies.

How to Contact a Lactation Consultant (IBCLC, RLC)

If you have access to an IBCLC, RLC at your hospital or doctor's office:

Call your hospital or pediatrician's office and ask to speak with the Lactation Consultant. If she is available, consult with her over the phone and/or schedule an appointment to be seen in person ASAP. If she is not quickly available, utilize this book and a breastfeeding hotline until you can meet with your IBCLC in person. For example, the Tennessee Breastfeeding Hotline is 855-4BF-MOMS and is available 24 hours a day, 7 days a week.

If you do not have access to an IBCLC, RLC at your hospital or doctor's office:

Use this book and a breastfeeding hotline until you can schedule a consult with an IBCLC in private practice. Ask your pediatrician to recommend an IBCLC or go to uslca.org and enter your zip code to find IBCLCs closest to you. If you are a WIC participant, contact your local health department. Let them know you are experiencing serious breastfeeding problems and need help immediately. Do not hesitate to call the National Helpline at 1-800-994-9662, which is available Monday – Friday from 9:00 am to 6:00 pm ET. An extensive listing of international helplines is available at kellymom.com.

A note about postpartum depression: If you find yourself overwhelmed, contact your healthcare provider without delay. Early postpartum sleep deprivation mixed with fluctuating hormones and strong emotions can develop into a state of mind that requires medical intervention. Do not hesitate to discuss how you are feeling with a medical professional right away.

Attention dads!

According to the Surgeon General of the United States, you are vital to breastfeeding success. Aside from the obvious need that a mother has to be cared for and encouraged, the 2011 Surgeon General's Call to Action to Support Breastfeeding cites numerous studies showing a direct correlation between a father's positive or negative influence and breastfeeding outcomes. If you're wondering how you can be a positive influence, help her keep in mind that she is the only who can make the milk – everything else can be done by everyone else. So ask mom what she needs, and if she says "nothing", put in a load of laundry and do the dishes while she nurses. That will be a powerful, non-verbal message that you support her.

Insurance Coverage

Many insurance plans will cover some lactation services and may also provide a breast pump of some kind. Remember that, if you are experiencing significant breastfeeding difficulties, you will likely need to rent a multiple-user large motor ("hospital grade") breast pump, at least for the short term. See **Right Pump for You** on page 40. Your insurance company may provide a small motor single-user pump designed for occasional use only, which may not be appropriate right away. During the critical first few weeks, obtain the highest quality pump you can afford so that you have the best opportunity to achieve your goals. Locate a rental station in your area or ask for rental information from the hospital where you delivered. **Renting a breast pump is less expensive than a month's worth of formula and is often the key to long term breastfeeding success**. If you cannot obtain a rental pump, a high quality manual breast pump, used in combination with breast massage, is a secondary option.

Abbreviations and Definitions

Gender – For the purposes of this book, mother will be referred to as "she" and baby will referred to as "he" to avoid confusion, not as a slight to baby girls!

Obstetrician (OB)– Mom's maternity health care provider (HCP). "Obstetrician" will be used to identify all maternity HCPs, such as a Certified Nurse Midwife (CNM) and Nurse Practitioner (NP).

Pediatrician – Baby's HCP. "Pediatrician" will be used to identify all pediatric HCPs, such as Nurse Practitioner (NP) or Physician Assistant (PA).

IBCLC, RLC – International Board Certified Lactation Consultant, Registered Lactation Consultant. IBCLC, RLC identifies the expert lactation care provider. Other breastfeeding helpers with different titles have a more limited scope of practice. In this book, the abbreviation IBCLC will be used.

The Bridge Generation – The current generation of new parents is caught between primarily formula-feeding generations, who had little to no breastfeeding support, and the coming generations who will have much greater support and view breastfeeding as the normal way to feed a baby. Therefore, this generation is the "bridge" and their culture tells them, "You really should breastfeed, but we can't help you and we don't want to see it." Sometimes breastmilk in bottles is the vehicle that can be used to navigate the generational bridge. Brave new parents are conquering many challenges, and their children will benefit from their efforts.

W h a t i s y o u r

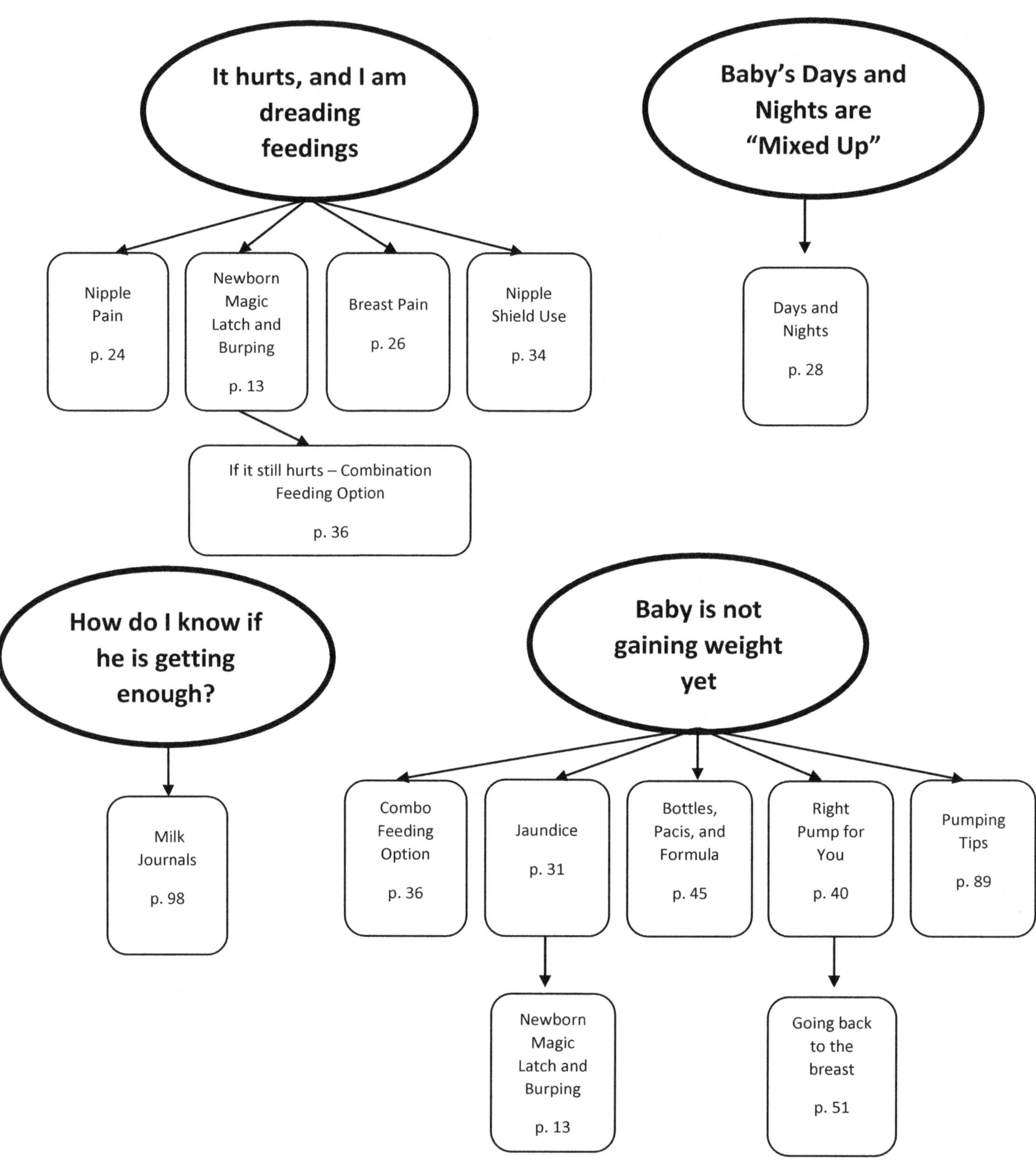
It hurts, and I am dreading feedings
Nipple Pain p. 24
Newborn Magic Latch and Burping p. 13
Breast Pain p. 26
Nipple Shield Use p. 34
If it still hurts – Combination Feeding Option p. 36
Baby's Days and Nights are "Mixed Up"
Days and Nights p. 28
How do I know if he is getting enough?
Milk Journals p. 98
Baby is not gaining weight yet
Combo Feeding Option p. 36
Jaundice p. 31
Bottles, Pacis, and Formula p. 45
Right Pump for You p. 40
Pumping Tips p. 89
Newborn Magic Latch and Burping p. 13
Going back to the breast p. 51

Breastfeeding Challenge?

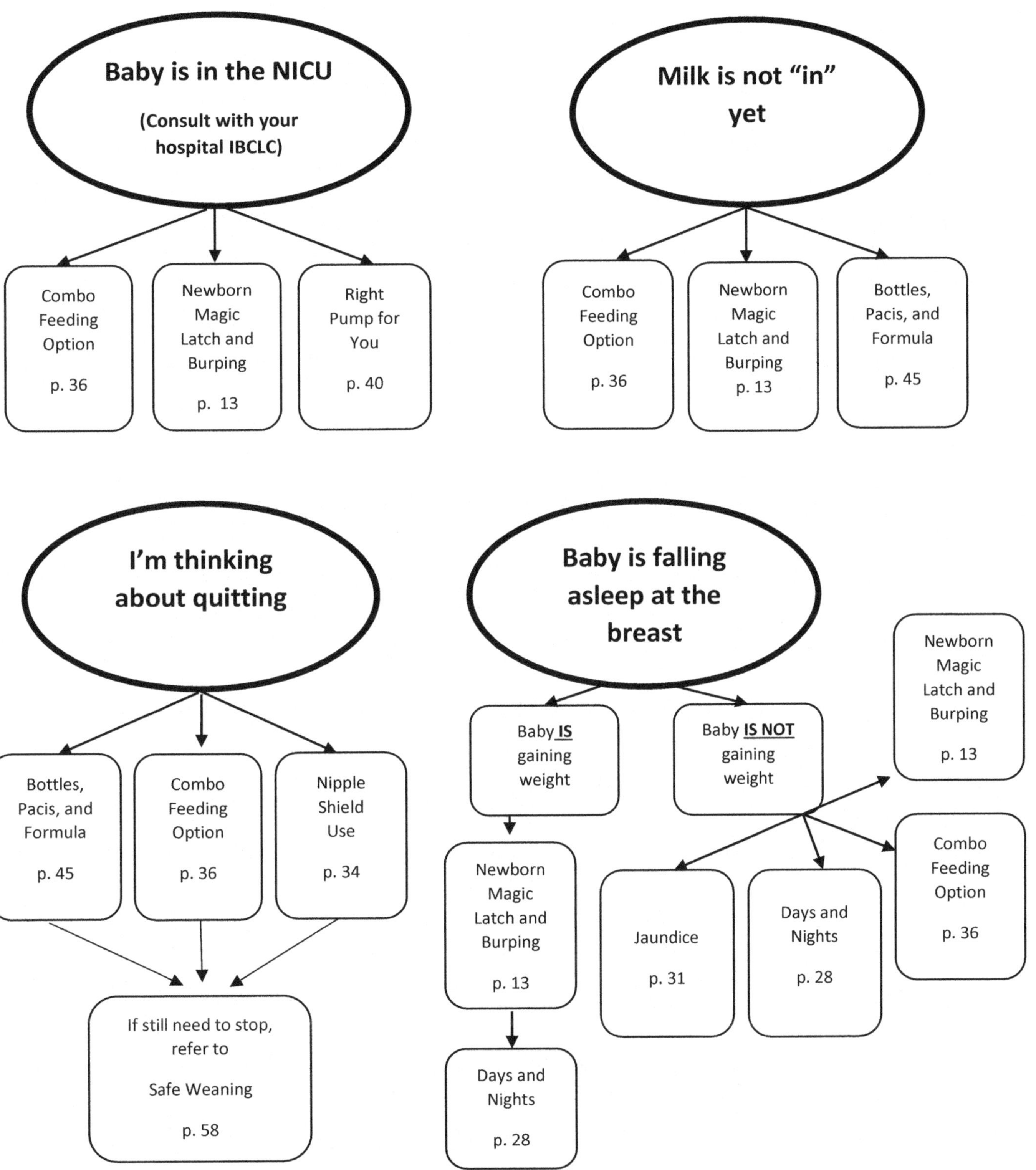

Part 2

Care Plans

Newborn Magic Latching and Burping

Using logic to help baby drink and burp

Video reference at nursingnook.com under Breastfeeding Help Videos

The difference between a newborn and an infant

The healthy, full term newborn will seek his food source and attach himself to it with minimal assistance. It's mom's job to make sure the attachment isn't painful for her and isn't limiting baby's ability to transfer milk. You may sense that the process is more natural to your baby, and often it is. But sometimes you have to "direct the traffic" by supporting your breast and supporting your baby. You could think of it this way: He gets to drive; his brain will tell him what to do, but you have to keep him in the road. In other words, until he gets a little older, he may not be able to get the breast where he needs it to be for a successful feeding. Older babies when brought to the breast are "old pros", and proper positioning and latching technique are things of the past. Your newborn needs time to learn and may need to have help getting his body lined up with yours so he can drink. Pretty soon you can hold him any way you want to and he will be able to drink. This is the way you've seen other mothers who have already survived the newborn period. But today he needs you to just help "keep him in the road".

Helping you discover your magic latch

If lactation care providers activate the left side of your brain (which is focused on details) by giving you multiple rules and multiple names for different breastfeeding positions, we can short-circuit your hardwiring for right-brained (big picture) mothering. We're doing our best to avoid doing that by instead encouraging mothers to position their babies more intuitively with the help of some pioneer researchers, like Dr. Suzanne Colson leading the way and Nancy Mohrbacher, IBCLC, continuing the quest.[1]

Instead of being focused on the details of what someone else tells you is a good latch, try seeing the bigger picture: If it doesn't hurt you and the baby is swallowing enough milk to keep pooping, it's a good latch. Just nurse. If it hurts, it shouldn't and something's not right. Get help.

Newborns require a little more maternal intervention during the learning process. Older babies have more head and neck control. They can breastfeed with minimal assistance. A full-term newborn is ready with reflexes to search for food, but because he doesn't know there is an easier way, he might latch on over his shoulders and suck with his head to the side (see photo below). It would be difficult for an adult to drink in that position. For the newborn, it's even more difficult. But even if milk isn't coming out, he'll still suck and chomp down on the breast, which can be painful for mom. You may be relieved that he is eating, so you allow this type of nursing until he falls asleep. Then, when you remove him from the breast, he wakes up and cries. This cycle can be intensely frustrating for new parents.

AVOID THIS POSITION

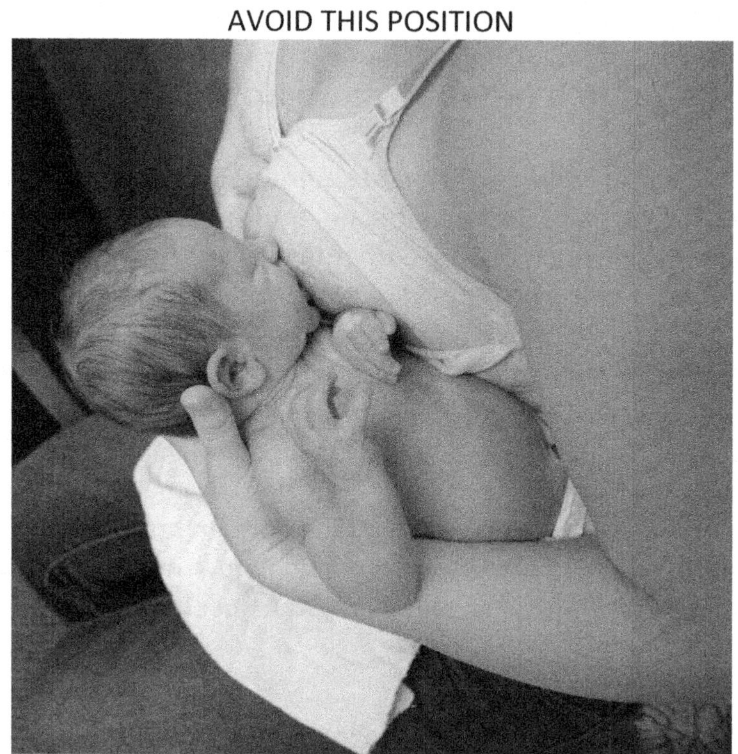

AVOID THIS POSITION

Older babies can sometimes nurse in this position because they know what to do. They know where they have to put their jaw to get the most milk. They have more control over their upper bodies which makes them able to move around to their own magic place on the breast. They have also found the spot that doesn't hurt their mothers either. **Newborns are designed to search for food; moms are designed to be sure they find it.**

When used with a newborn, the position above typically hurts mom because he tends to chew the front of mom's nipple instead of suckling behind her nipple and "drinking" from the breast. Even if someone tells you his latch looks ok, remember that's only 50% of the equation. The other 50% is what's going on inside the baby's mouth. And nursing in this position might not give him as many calories since the milk isn't releasing well due to compression of the nipple. Eventually, the compression of the nipple causes mom significant amounts of pain and puts her at risk for infection. What can we do about that?

Think drink. In what kind of position would your body, neck, head, mouth, and nose need to be before you could drink properly? You sure wouldn't do well if you had to drink over your shoulder with your head tilted down. If you feel like you're battling your baby at the breast, something's not right. Don't continue to battle because you've been told to do it that way. Follow your instincts.

Here's the big picture: The general problem with the old method is the concept of "taking the breast to the baby", like you would take the bottle to the baby. The general solution in the new method is to "bring the baby to the breast". The challenge in making the new method work is ensuring mom's comfort. One of the reasons moms tend to "take the breast to the baby" is to protect their lower back. To bring the baby to the breast, mom must first be comfortable. She needs anti-gravity aids. One example of a comfortable breastfeeding position is the "Natural Breastfeeding Position". **See Dr. Theresa Nesbitt and Nancy Mohrbacher's website for more information and videos.**[2]

If you would rather nurse in a more upright position, other anti-gravity aids are nursing pillows and foot stools. Again, the type matters. The My Breastfriend ™ pillow fastens around you and provides stable support. Pillows that fall away from your body can make latching more difficult and less comfortable. Choose a foot stool that is slanted and grooved so you can push against it while nursing in a chair or rocker. My Brestfriend ™ retails this type of nursing stool that can also be adjusted to use as a kids' bathroom stool later.

The new research reveals what we should have known all along: we've been making this too hard. **We've been trying to breastfeed in bottle feeding positions.** Crazy. Time for logic. The following information is the long version of "think drink". It sheds light on things from the baby's perspective. It's not a long set of rules; it's a reminder of basic ergonomics and a knowledge of the way babies are "hardwired to breastfeed".[1] Just put yourself in his shoes. Could you drink if your cup was over your shoulder or below your mouth?

Picture how you would need to be positioned to drink from a cup. Try leaning back, getting yourself comfortable first, then place your baby chest-to-chest with you.

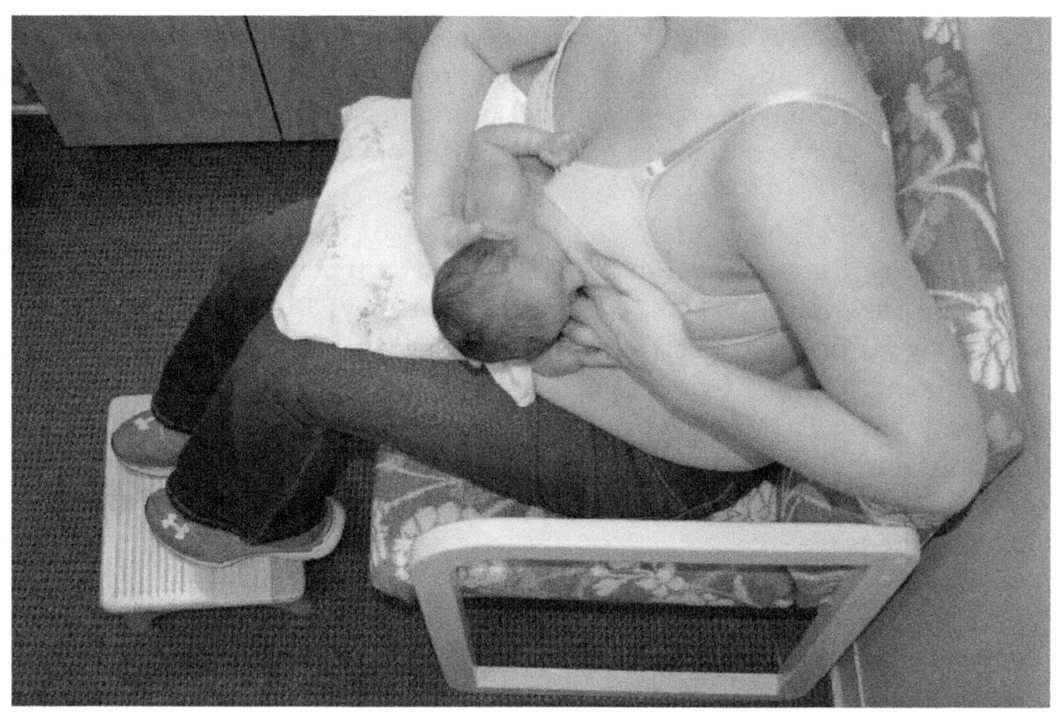

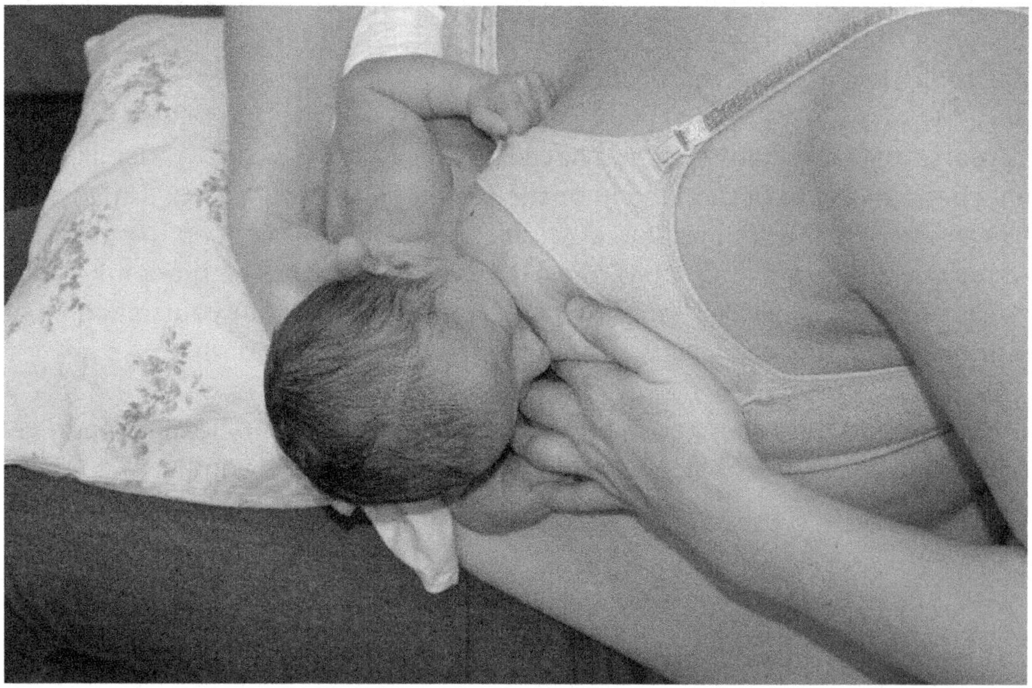

When there is no distance between your chest and his, two things happen. First, he feels more secure and doesn't need to suck his hands for comfort. Second, he's close enough to latch on to your breast more deeply and comfortably for both of you. If you're worried about his breathing, tuck your elbow into your side, which moves his bottom closer to your body. That should open up his face and clear some space around his nostrils.

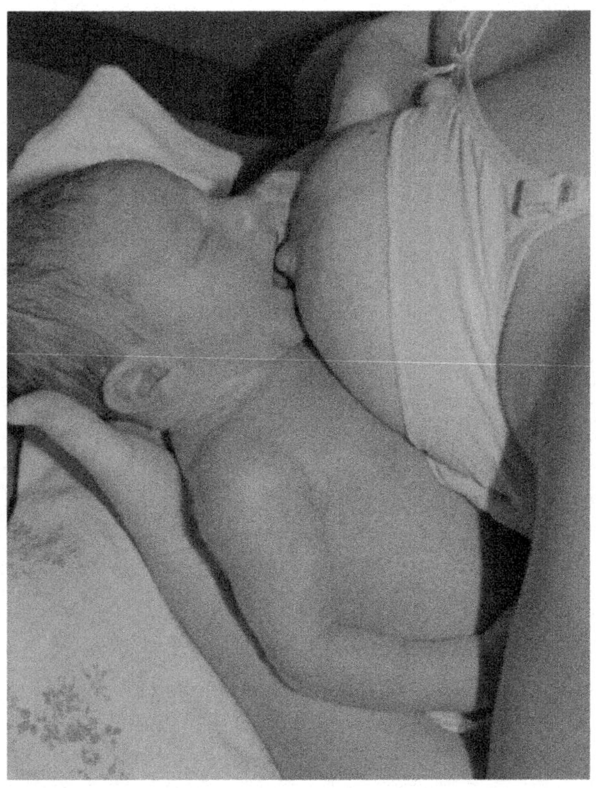

When his body is aligned, he won't have to twist and drink at the same time.

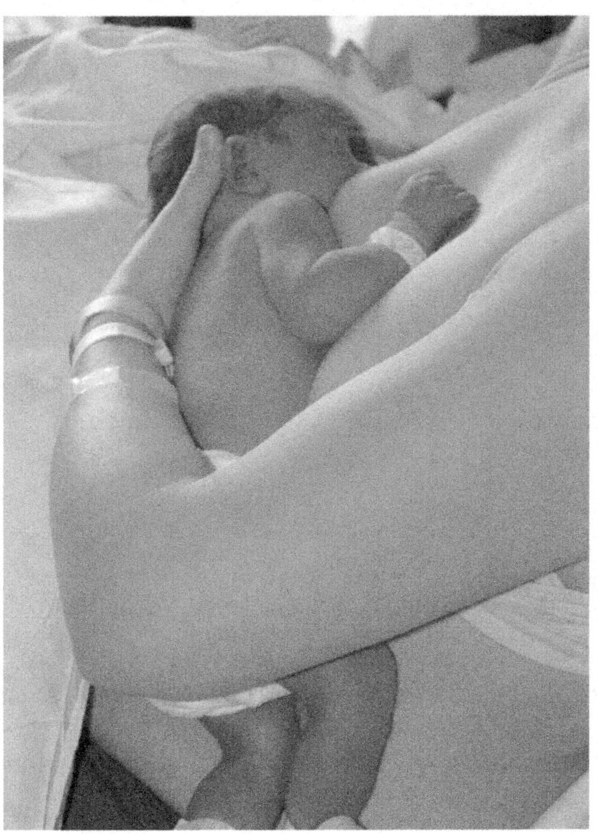

When his arms are around your breast instead of tucked beside his body, he'll be happier. His body was flexed in utero, so that feels right and safe to him. In this position, he won't have to nurse over his shoulder.

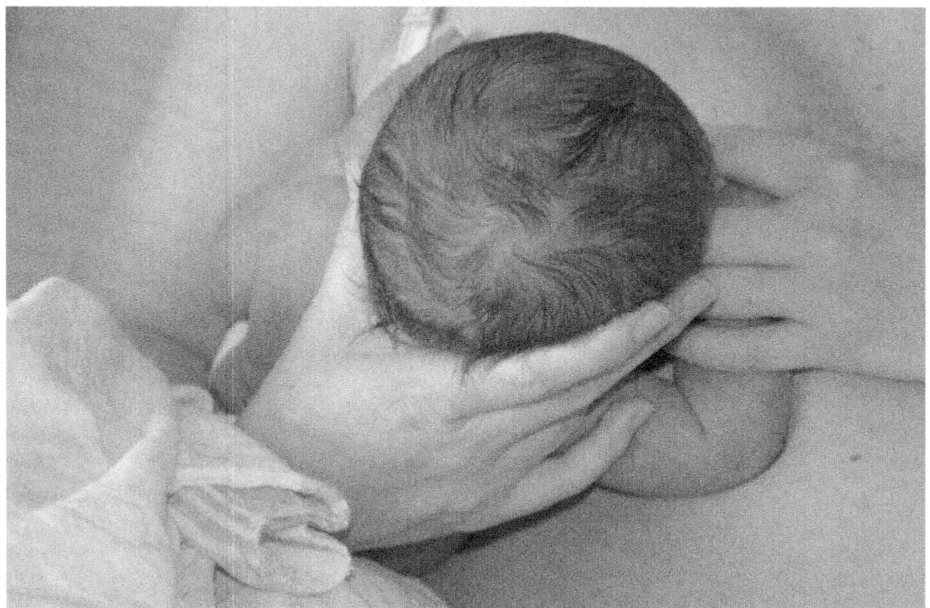

With your hand at the base of his skull, rather than the back of his head, he can tip his head back for drinking instead of having to nurse with his chin and mouth in a downward position.

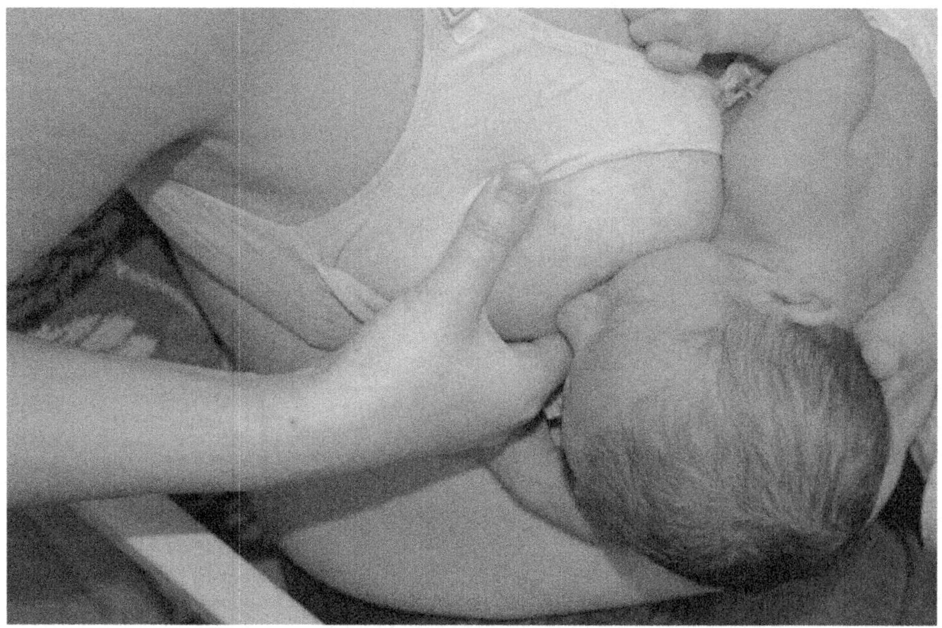

Because you are supporting your breast with your free hand, he won't be forced to tuck his chin in order to follow your nipple.

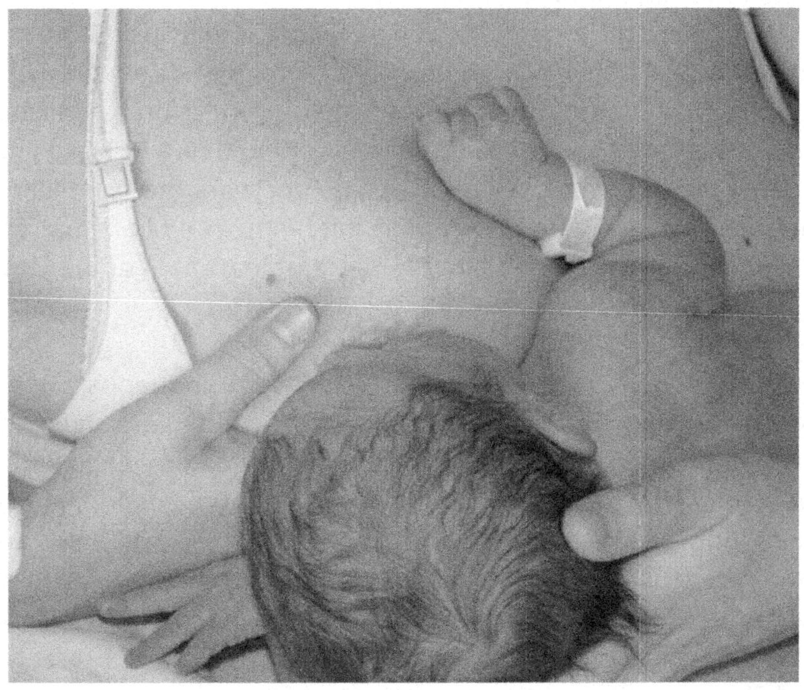

With your nipple lined up with his nose instead of his mouth, his chin will touch your breast first, and he can organize himself better. This also places his bottom gum well below the nipple. He will latch on more deeply, which will be more comfortable for you and more rewarding for him. Mohrbacher and Kendall-Tackett call this "finding the comfort zone".[1] The odds of finding it are better when you work with your bodies instead of against them.

Latching your baby to the breast doesn't take this much effort forever. This would not be the mammal feeding plan if it was constantly difficult. You won't always need to consciously "think drink" before latching your baby to the breast. Pleasurable feedings at the breast develop memories in his brain. He will start comfortably latching automatically. But in the first couple of weeks, checking to be sure you've achieved a comfortable drinking position for both of you is key. It might be the difference between going down the difficult road and going down the easier road.

If the latching videos on nursingnook.com and naturalbreastfeeding.com aren't working for you, there are other latching options. The third chapter in *Breastfeeding Made Simple* by Nancy Mohrbacher and Kathleen Kendall-Tackett beautifully illustrates in detail how to achieve a comfortable and effective latch in several different positions.[1]

If you have given your baby an opportunity to latch onto the breast in a way that he is able to drink comfortably and you're still in pain, try using a nipple shield. See **Nipple Shield Use** page 34. If you continue to have significant discomfort, it's ok to limit direct breastfeeding as long as you have a rental pump. See **Right Pump for You** page 40. Focus on establishing and maintaining your milk supply to buy you some time. Work with an IBCLC to figure out what's going on with your latching challenges. There may be something that's making it more difficult for you to reach this goal. For example, if mom has flat nipples and baby has a tongue tie, it is a challenge to achieve a comfortable, deep latch. See **Combination Feeding Option** page 36, **Nipple Pain** page 24, and **Breast Pain** page 26.

A word about multiples: It's logical to want to nurse twins simultaneously to save time, but it can be risky for their intake and your milk supply, especially if they are sleepy or jaundiced. Newborns require more postural support than a new mother can manage with one hand.[3] Sequential feeding (nursing one at a time) can work better in the beginning. Newborn twins nearly always require mom to "preserve lactation with pumping" until twins are aged past their due date.[3] When they are truly "full term", they are ready to work for "full feeds" at breast. Again, **a maximized milk supply is the best protection for a successful transition to feeding directly from the breast**. It's particularly important for mothers of multiples to consult early and often with an IBCLC.

Key concepts:

- Good latch = decreased pain and increased drain
- Soft breasts and a happy baby after each feeding = sign that milk is transferring well
- Newborns are designed to search for food; moms are designed to make sure they find it.

References

1. Mohrbacher N, Kendall-Tackett K. *Breastfeeding Made Simple* 2010: 15.
2. www.naturalbreastfeeding.com. Accessed February 2018.
3. Wilson-Clay B, Hoover K. *The Breastfeeding Atlas* 2017: 109-111.

Magic Newborn Burping

Video reference at nursingnook.com under Breastfeeding Help Videos

An older baby will sense when he needs to burp, unlatch himself from the breast, burp, look up into your eyes, smile at you, and re-latch himself to continue drinking comfortably. Not so with your newborn. Today he will latch onto anything (including dad's arm), regardless of whether milk is coming out or not. He's designed for sucking; you're designed to direct him toward sucking that will result in a feeding. If he is latched to your breast and receiving any milk whatsoever, he doesn't yet know there is a second breast and may keep going and going and going even when there isn't milk coming out. Often this results in his pacifying himself to sleep. This is called "non-nutritive" sucking. It will look like quick bursts of shallow sucks with long pauses in between.

You don't yet know how much milk is in each breast, so he may have just gulped down 2 ounces of milk without a burp. Unless you remove him from the breast early and often, he'll do one of two things. Either he'll eventually burp the air up and bring up some milk with it (spit up), or he'll not burp the air up, and it goes down a long journey to the other end (gas).

A note about newborn gas: All adults pass gas, and it's not always because of something we ate. It can be because we breathed and swallowed at the same time. In the same way, babies pass gas, and it's **not** always because of something they or their mothers ate. Babies have guts that are immature like everything else about them. And, while the gut is practicing moving, the air moves. **Gas is good. It is proof that your baby's gut is activated**.

Burping is different before the mature milk comes in. Until your baby is gulping air and milk at the same time, he may not need to burp at all. Colostrum is wonderfully thick in texture. In fact, it is the perfect thickness for practice sucking, swallowing, and breathing in that order.[1] When swallowing thick colostrum, your baby might suck several times before he swallows. He has to actively suck colostrum and is in charge of the flow. Not much burping is needed before the mature milk comes in because not much gulping happens until the mature milk arrives. Your mature milk is larger in volume and faster in flow which means he has to keep up with the flow by gulping sometimes. And that's when he starts to swallow air. The same is the case with gulping from a bottle. Gulping air = needing to burp occasionally.

So, when to burp? You may have been told to burp the baby "between the sides", meaning to nurse one breast, burp the baby, nurse the other breast, burp again. That's fine if all women had the same volume of milk available at each feeding and every baby ate with the same aggression. They don't. Some women "store" an ounce or two per breast at one time; some women store six ounces per breast at one time. So, when your baby stops nursing and wiggles around a little-- even if he hasn't been nursing more than 2-3 minutes-- go ahead and unlatch him. He may have already had 2 ounces and, at this age, you wouldn't let him have that much from a bottle without stopping to burp him.

Pain prevention alert: When interrupting a newborn's latch, remember to slide your finger inside the corner of his mouth and break the suction between his gums before you let him come off your breast. This will prevent him from damaging your nipples while trying to hang on for more as you pull him off - ouch!

Sit him upright on your lap and tuck him close to you. Support the weight of his head with one hand while supporting his back with the other. Wrap your fingers around his hip and place your thumb on his spine for support. Gently straighten his back, lifting the pressure of his head and rib cage off his stomach. **Just hold him there for 15-30 seconds**. No need to pat or rub; just allow the air to bubble up around the milk. Back to ergonomics: think about your body posture when you need to burp. Do you lift your rib cage off your stomach so that the air can escape?

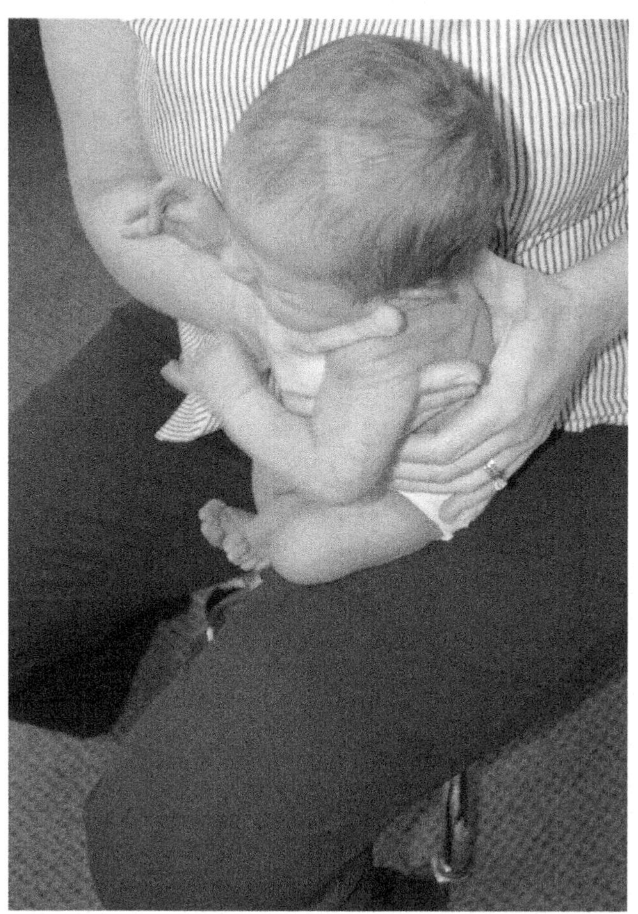

If this doesn't release the swallowed air, lean your baby back on your lap and roll him slowly from one side to the other. Then sit him up and try one more time. If he still doesn't burp in a **maximum time of 60 seconds**, let him keep nursing and try again in a bit. This position helps to quicken the burp and lessen the spit-up due to decreased pressure on the stomach. As always and no matter what, do what works for you. If this suggestion doesn't work, do whatever feels natural to you.

The key with newborn burping is not to spend several minutes trying to get him to burp. He might fall asleep and not return to the breast. He has limited alert time (see **Days and Nights** page 28). If he drinks until he's not hungry, but doesn't drink until he's full, he's likely to awaken in 15-30 minutes and ask for a little more. Of course, that's ok and you should answer his call for more food, but these suggestions may help both of you to rest more.

By the way, expect him to start sucking again when you attempt to unlatch him from the breast. He wants to keep sucking for comfort. Assess whether he is still hungry or not by his behavior after coming off the breast. Are his arms relaxed or are his hands in his mouth? Is he drowsy or restless? If his arms are relaxed and he is drowsy or asleep, you can assume he was just sucking for comfort. If the opposite is true, you can put him back to the breast and massage the breast while he is nursing to help him transfer more milk.

"Grazing", or snack feeding, is not a problem for him. He'd rather not work for his food anyway. He would prefer to return to the passive nutrition he enjoyed in utero. Eating a little, sleeping a little, eating a little works just fine for him. It may become a problem for you, however, because your breasts may be very full and you need for him to be more alert during feedings. Or the opposite may be true. Your breasts may not be making large volumes of milk yet, and you need him to stimulate more production. Either way, give him a brief opportunity to burp. If he doesn't burp and certainly if he's crying, go ahead and put him back on the same breast for additional nursing until that breast feels much softer to you. Try to burp again later when he's restless or stops swallowing. He may be giving you the subtle signal that he's a little uncomfortable; he doesn't know why, and he would like you to do something about it.

Now, after all those suggestions, here's the main thing: **Don't obsess over burping**. As the days go by, you will learn his little signals, and your dance will become easier with practice. If the air brings some milk with it, and he spits enough to cover his chin and drip down on your hand, that's usually only a milliliter or two of milk. It just looks like a lot more. "Wet burps" are normal. If he is spitting up with a lot of force and the spit up shoots out from his body into a big splat on the floor, that's called "projectile vomiting". If he does that more than once in a 24-hour period, take him to be examined by his pediatrician because that's a whole different ball game.

There are many approaches to latching a baby to the breast and helping a baby burp. Again, do what is working for you! These are just suggestions based on the author's experience in practice.

Reference

Genna C, Sandora L. Supporting Sucking Skills 2013; 7.

Nipple Pain

Direct breastfeeding

How you position yourself and baby before you start the latch is of highest importance. Your body should be supported so that your neck, shoulders, and back aren't strained during the feeding. Lean back and let gravity help you. Start each feeding on the **less painful side first** due to newborn's more aggressive suck to obtain initial let-down of milk. Remember to **"think drink"** when bringing baby to breast – how would your body be positioned if you were the one drinking? Refer to **Newborn Magic Latch and Burping** page 13 for more information.

Using a nipple shield

If position adjustment does not relieve your pain, nursing with a Medela brand nipple shield over your nipple may help. Work with your IBCLC. You may have to experiment with which size shield works best. During the early weeks of breastfeeding, it is strongly recommended that you pump after nursing to make sure breasts are drained. Drained breasts tell the body to keep making milk. This also helps prevent breast infection. Your baby will need regular weight checks until he is able to nurse without the shield. Refer to **Nipple Shield Use** page 34 for more information.

Pumping milk from your breasts

If nursing is too painful, breast drainage with a **multiple-user rental breast pump** is the best choice for effective and comfortable milk removal. Draining your breasts 8-12 times every 24 hours in the first 2 weeks is essential for establishment and maintenance of milk supply, as well as to reduce risk of severe breast engorgement and infection. It is normal for each breast to produce a different volume of milk.[1] Expressing your milk with a manual or a single-user, small motor pump (for example a pump that was provided by your insurance) may be utilized for a short time in the event of inability to obtain a rental pump. However, if you use a single-user pump, you will need frequent follow up with your IBCLC. Transition back to breast ASAP. If pumping is uncomfortable, check for proper breast shield fit and decrease the suction on the pump until you are comfortable.[2] See **Right Pump for You** page 40, **Proper Breast Flange Fit** page 88, **Pumping Tips** page 89, **Combination Feeding Option** page 36, and **Going Back to the Breast** page 51.

Pain relieving medicine

The anti-inflammatory pain relieving medicine, **Ibuprofen** (brand names Motrin, Advil), is preferred during breastfeeding due to its safety rating.[3,4] Very little of the medicine, if any, crosses into breast milk. Ibuprofen is able to relieve pain as well as reduce inflammation. If you are currently taking Naproxen Sodium (brand names Anaprox, Aleve), you can ask your obstetrician to change your prescription to Ibuprofen. Take one or the other, but not both.

Nipple skin care

Daily washing of nipples will help limit bacteria on skin and prevent infection. Gently wash your nipples with soap and water once daily. Application of expressed breast milk, which has anti-microbial properties, is helpful to rub into your nipples after nursing. Other **topical agents** can also promote wound healing. Check with your health care provider as needed. Also check your personal allergies before using:

- ☐ **Coconut oil or Olive oil**
  regular food grade – apply before pumping and/or following nursing

- ☐ **Non-lanolin-based, over-the-counter nipple ointment**
  apply before pumping and/or following nursing

And if you have broken skin (especially if bleeding or scabs):

- ☐ **Triple antibiotic ointment**-- available over the counter, but check your allergies.
  After nursing or pumping, apply 3 times daily x 3 days only and meet with your IBCLC

Probiotics

If you were given IV antibiotics during labor or following a C-section, probiotics might help prevent nipple and breast yeast infection. There are several formulations for infants as well as adults. Ask your pediatrician and obstetrician to recommend one for each of you. Also, moms, you can eat yogurt daily to replenish your beneficial bacteria.

Call your obstetrician with any symptoms of infection or persistent pain.
Also contact your IBCLC.

References

1. Engstrom J, Meier P, Jegier B, et al. Comparison of milk output from the right and left breasts during simultaneous pumping in mothers of very low birthweight infants. *Breastfeeding Medicine* 2007:2(2):83-91.
2. Kent JC, Mitoulas LR, Cregan MD, Geddes DT, Larsson M, Doherty DA, Hartmann PE. Importance of vacuum for milk expression. *Breastfeeding Medicine* 2008 Mar;3(1):11-19.
3. Reece-Stremtan S, Campos M, Kokajko L, and the Academy of Breastfeeding Medicine. *Breastfeeding Medicine*. November 2017,12(9):500-506.
4. Weibert R, Townsend R, Kaiser D, et al. Lack of ibuprofen secretion into human milk. *Clin Pharm* 1982;1:457-458.

Breast Pain

TREATMENT- GET THE SWELLING DOWN AND THE MILK OUT

↓

Apply warm compress to the breasts for 2-3 minutes

↓

Lie on your back and use your fingers to press inward on the areola around the nipple. See photos on next page.

↓

Try to latch baby (5 minutes)

BABY LATCHES WELL

↓

If baby latches well, feed on that breast until softer. Use gentle breast massage and compression during the feeding. Switch sides after the first side is softer. If baby is not interested in nursing the second side and you are uncomfortable, you can hand express or pump briefly for comfort. Start on this side for the next feeding. Lie down and rest between nursing session to help decrease swelling.

BABY CANNOT LATCH

↓

If baby cannot latch, try hand expression or pumping to start the release of milk.

↓

When the milk starts dripping, try to latch baby (5 minutes)

↓

If baby latches well, follow instructions on the left side of the chart.

↓

If baby cannot latch, then pump breasts one at a time until comfortable and no more than 20 min. A multiple-user rental breastpump may be necessary if you are unable to resolve your breastpain. See **Right Pump for You** page 40.

↓

If breasts are still firm after pumping, lie down and apply ice packs for 20 minutes. Optional: Place a green cabbage leaf in your bra until wilted, then repeat until milk is releasing well.

↓

Start the process again every 2 hours (or more often if needed) until the breasts are soft and comfortable. If not improving with the above steps, see **Plugged Milk Duct and Mastitis** page 56 and call your OB. Typically breast engorgement is limited to a just a few days.

Sometime between the second and fifth day after your baby is born, your milk will change from colostrum to mature milk. During this time, most women notice some heaviness and/or warmth, which is normal. However, breast edema or engorgement occurs when the breasts are not drained properly. The breasts become very full, hard, and painful. This can cause the baby not to latch properly. In early breastfeeding, it is not typically a sign of too much milk, but is actually excess blood-flow and fluid buildup in the breasts. If engorgement is severe and not relieved quickly, milk can be trapped by swelling, and mom's milk supply could be reduced.[1] **Lie down as much as possible** to help decrease breast swelling.

Important note: **Ibuprofen** is the preferred medication for pain and inflammation during breastfeeding.[2]

References

1. Berens P, Brodribb W, and the Academy of Breastfeeding Medicine. *Breastfeeding Medicine*. May 2016, 11(4):159-163.
2. Reece-Stremtan S, et al, and the Academy of Breastfeeding Medicine. *Breastfeeding Medicine*. Nov 2017, 12(9):500-506

Reverse Pressure Softening and Cabbage Use

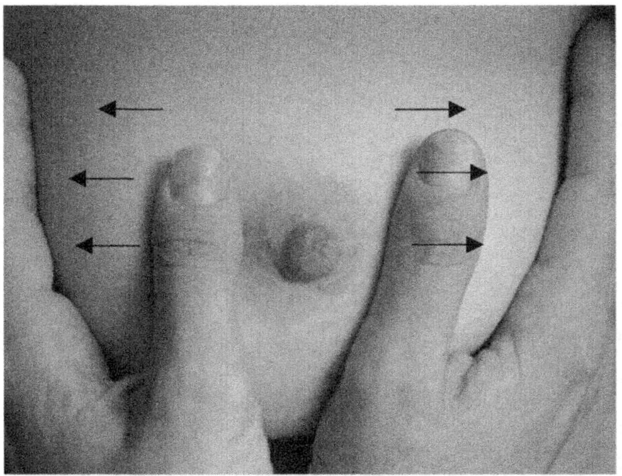

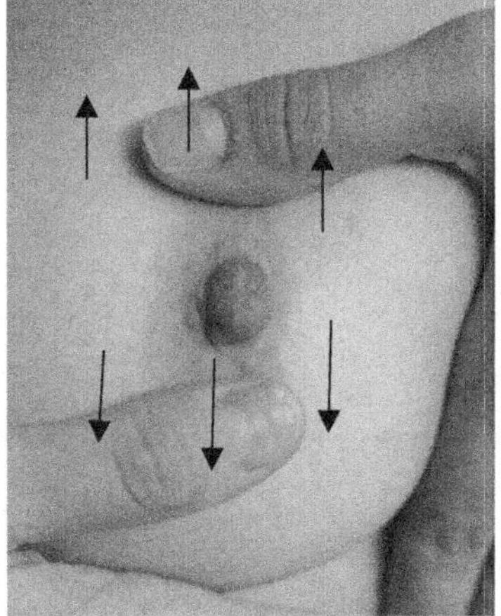

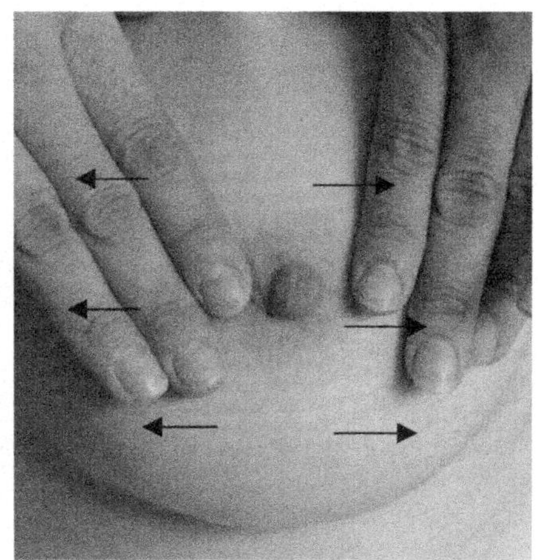

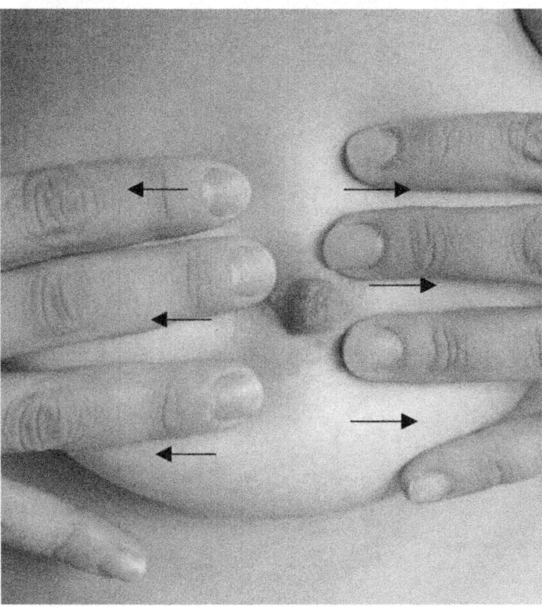

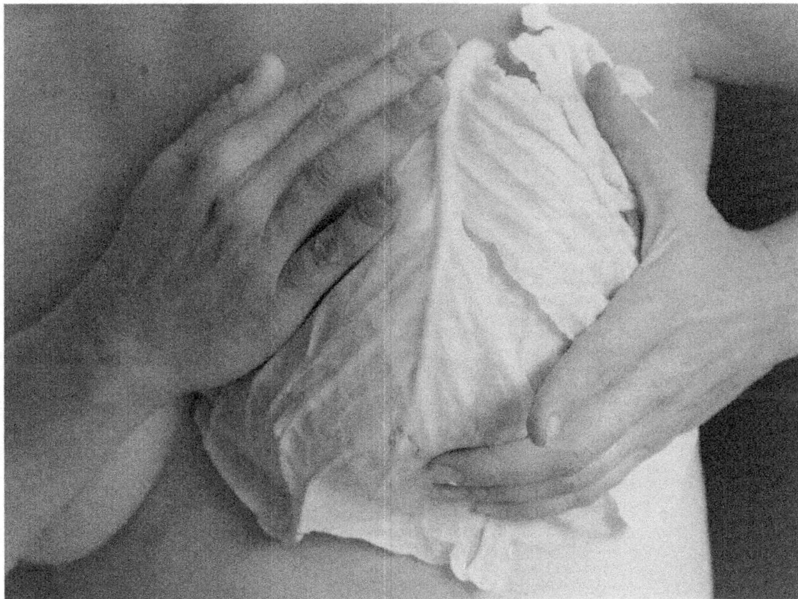

Days and Nights

*For baby's **first month** of life, try this daytime rhythm for more alert daytime feeds and better nighttime sleep.*

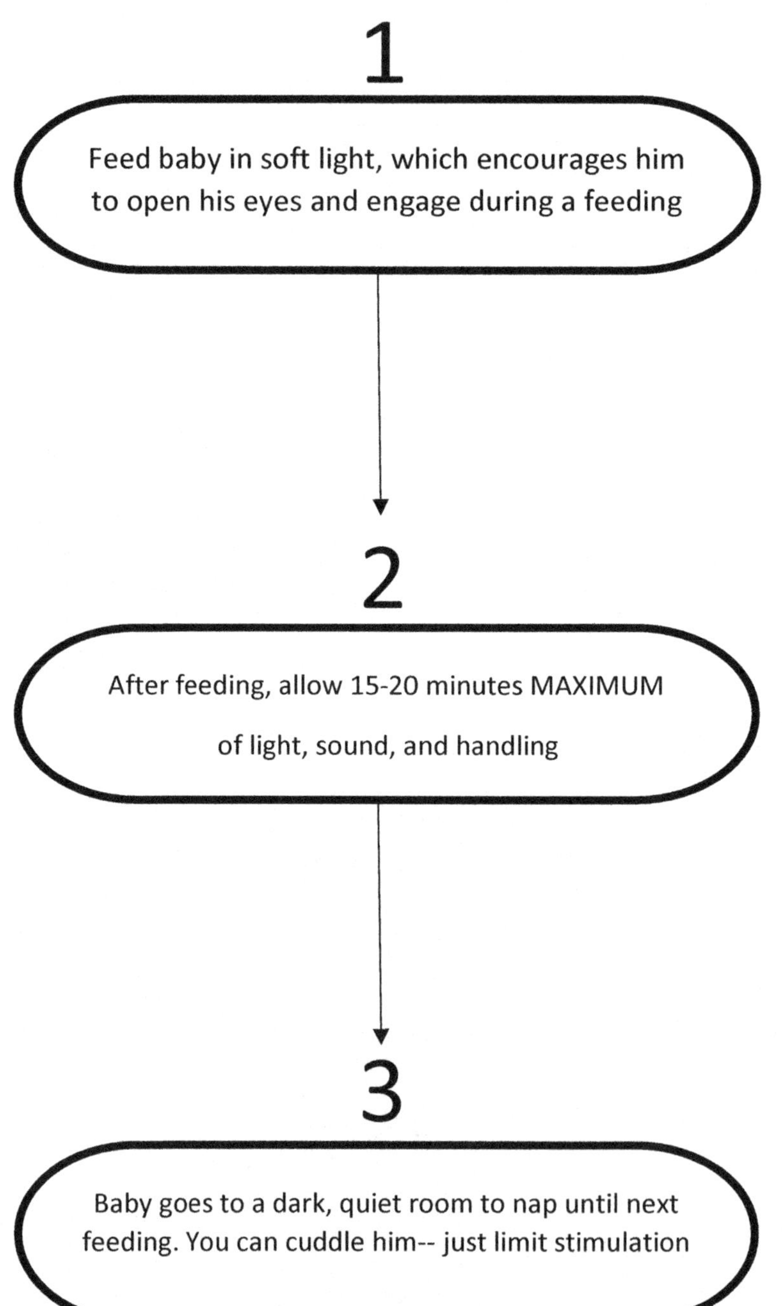

Days and Nights Mixed Up

What to do if baby is "sleepy" during daytime feedings and "wide awake" at night

Facts about newborns

- Newborns need about **16 hours** of sleep every 24 hours.[1] They sleep 8-9 hours at night and 8 hours during the day, and are supposed to eat around the clock.[2]
- "Breastfeeding success is affected by the behavior of the newborn".[3] You cannot force a baby to nurse well. Deep sleep first; alert feeding second.
- The more you protect the baby's days, the more the baby protects your nights.

Better Sleeping = Better Feeding

- Keep visitors to a minimum throughout your hospital stay and at home. If needed, enlist the help of the nurses and close family members to accomplish this. You will be up at night; your visitors will not. You must protect your daytime rest as well as the baby's. Just like you feel when you've slept in the living room with the lights and TV on, **lights, sounds, and handling** can overwhelm your baby and can cause him to shut down and appear **sleepy and disinterested in feeding.**[4] Then at night when the world is quiet, darker, and he is not being handled, deeper sleep is more possible for him. And just like you wake up refreshed and ready to function after a good stretch of deep sleep, he will awake more alert and ready to feed after a time of quiet rest during the day.

- The lack of deep, restorative sleep during the newborn's **DAY** starts the domino effect of "shut-down-sleeping" followed by sleepy feeding all day, and then deep sleep followed by alert feeding all night. Hence the phrase, "the baby's days and nights are mixed up".

- Maximize daytime feedings, which helps baby gain weight and eliminate jaundice, in addition to keeping mom comfortable. Provide more opportunities for "nighttime-quality" sleep during the day. This also sets up the daytime rhythm for **deep sleep first, alert feeding second**. Babies are supposed to eat during the night.

- In the first few weeks of life – most especially in the first few days – it's worth the effort to limit the stimulation of baby. Alert feeds and good sleep are helped by limiting lights, sounds, and handling of baby to a maximum of **15-20 minutes after the daytime feedings**. Total time including feeding, burping, diapering, plus daytime playtime is about an hour. This is the ideal time to allow older siblings to hold and talk to the baby. You can refer to it as their special time. Avoid stimulation after night feedings, of course.

- If your pediatrician recommends indirect sunlight exposure to help decrease jaundice, you can do this as directed by your pediatrician. You may want to limit the light exposure to the 20 minutes after a feeding. (No matter how much sunlight exposure baby has, jaundice elimination requires good feedings followed by good poops.) Good feedings increase milk intake which enables baby to more quickly poop out components that cause jaundice. Alert feedings require good sleep. See **Breastfeeding during Jaundice** on page 31 for more information.

- Be watching for avoidance cues like yawns and **hiccoughs** (hiccups), which can be an indication that baby is overstimulated.[5,6] If baby starts to hiccough, it's time to let him rest. So, after the maximum stimulation time period of about 20 minutes, allow the baby to sleep in a darkened, quiet room – **not the living room** -- until the next feeding. Brightly lit bedrooms might benefit from room darkening shades. A more nighttime-type environment provides the opportunity for deeper sleep, hopefully followed by a higher quality feeding.

- If baby is restless or fussy, skin-to-skin contact with mom or just holding during the sleep time in the dark, quiet place can be very helpful. The trick is not to be on your phone, watching TV, playing music, or talking while holding the baby since **all of these things are stimulating** to the baby's brain, **even if he appears to be asleep**. The simple step of decreasing light and sound may allow him to organize and be more able to nurse.[7] If he is interested in nursing again, that's good. He may just need a little more milk.

- Important note: Anyone who wants to hold the baby between feedings (grandparents, for example) can cuddle the baby while he sleeps. Just stay in the dark and quiet location.

- The secret to the entire 24-hour strategy is the **quality of the daytime sleep**. Although counterintuitive, when we consider the immature newborn neurological system, it makes sense. If it feels like you are battling your baby to stay awake for feeds during the day and begging him to stay asleep between his feeds during the night, then maybe you are working against his brain instead of with it.

- **More restful sleep during the day = more restful sleep during the night**.

- General rule regarding visitors in the first 30 days: If the visitor is there to help you, good. If the visitor is there to "visit" with you, causing you not to rest, not good. That **daytime rest is essential** to the recovery of mother and protection of baby. Don't feel guilty about protecting your rest! You won't always have to be this protective. As you recover from childbirth and as the baby's neurological system matures, both of you will be able to do well with less daytime sleep.

References

1. Paruthi S, et al. Recommended amount of sleep for Pediatric Populations: A Statement of the Academy of Sleep Medicine. *J Clin Sleep Med*. 2016 May 25.
2. Infant Sleep. www.stanfordchildrens.org. Accessed Feb 2018.
3. Reece-Stremtan S, et al. *Breastfeeding Medicine*. Nov 2017;12(9):500-506.
4. Genna C, Nyqvist K. *Supporting Sucking Skills* 2013; 177, 184.
5. Als H, et al. Individualized developmental care for the vlbw infant. *JAMA* 1994;272:853-858
6. Wilson-Clay B, Hoover K. *The Breastfeeding Atlas* 2017: 8.
7. Genna C, Barak D. *Supporting Sucking Skills* 2013; 290, 292, 300.

Breastfeeding during Jaundice

If my baby is jaundiced, can I still breastfeed? Yes! Typically, MORE breast milk is needed to flush the jaundice from your baby's system. You can pump for a few minutes after the baby nurses and offer extra breast milk to your baby during this time if needed.

Is it normal for babies to be very sleepy when they are jaundiced? Yes. We don't know exactly why, but some jaundiced babies are so sleepy that they will sleep too long between feedings and fall asleep easily during feedings.[1] Make sure your baby has at least 8 feedings every 24 hours. If your baby is too sleepy to nurse enough to gain weight, see **Days and Nights** page 28 and **Combination Feeding Option** page 36.

What is the best way to protect breastfeeding during this time? Jaundice only lasts a few days for most newborns. There are more specifics below. In general, until jaundice resolves, the priorities are:

1. **Feed the baby.** Breast and bottle if necessary.
2. **Protect the milk supply.** Pump after nursing or instead of nursing, if necessary.
3. **Protect the breastfeeding relationship.** Nurse a few minutes if both of you are stable and able. Ask someone else to bottle feed his supplement while you pump. Return to exclusive breastfeeding as soon as you're both ready. See **Going Back to the Breast** page 51.

If our pediatrician advises us to feed infant formula to the baby, should I pump my breasts too? Yes. If your baby needs formula, your breasts need a pump. If your baby is not gaining weight well and/or needs extra milk to help him get rid of jaundice, your body could use some help establishing and maintaining your milk supply during these few days. Pump briefly after each nursing while someone else is offering the baby his extra milk. The sooner you start pumping and offering your milk as the extra milk, the less formula your baby will need. The type of breast pump you use during this time matters, especially if the baby is not nursing well for any reason. See **Right Pump for You** page 40.

Does it matter what kind of formula we use? Yes. Most formulas are fine to use, but The Academy of Breastfeeding Medicine has recommended that extensively hydrolyzed dairy protein formulas, such as Enfamil's Nutramigen and Similac's Alimentum, are preferable because they "avoid exposure to intact cow's milk proteins and reduce bilirubin levels [jaundice] more rapidly".[2] Research has shown specifically that Nutramigen helps eliminate jaundice more quickly.[3-7]

How do babies get jaundiced? More than 80% of all full term healthy newborns will develop visible jaundice.[8] It is usually harmless and goes away within a few days. All babies are born with extra red blood cells. When the baby's liver begins to break them down, a yellow pigment called bilirubin is produced. Bilirubin seeps from the baby's blood into his skin. The amount of bilirubin in his blood can be determined with a blood sample from your baby's heel. Jaundice is eliminated from your baby's body through his poop, so effective breastfeeding will help him get rid of jaundice. Ineffective breastfeeding, caused by poor latch or sleepy, infrequent feedings can result in a higher bilirubin level in your baby's blood. Some babies, such as premature babies (babies born more than 2 weeks early), babies with excessive bruising, or babies of diabetic mothers can be at higher risk for jaundice.

How do we get rid of jaundice? Feed the baby. Your baby's individual treatment plan will depend upon several factors, including how many days old your baby is in relation to how high his bilirubin blood level is. The most important aspect of the plan is to feed the baby. Bilirubin has to be pooped out of the gut, so without lots of milk, there's not lots of poop. Protecting the baby's rest so that he can breastfeed effectively is vital (see **Days and Nights** page 28). If your baby won't awake enough to eat well, offering extra breast milk or formula in a bottle becomes necessary. Don't worry about this temporary situation. Just protect your milk supply until the baby becomes more alert and is ready for primetime again (see **Combination Feeding Option** page 36 and **Going Back to the Breast** page 51). Remember, if your baby was a good nurser prior to jaundice, that's who he really is; he will be a good nurser again. If extra feeding doesn't keep the bilirubin level in the normal range, your baby may need phototherapy (see below).

What do the bilirubin numbers mean? Your pediatrician will explain these on a daily basis, as needed. But in general, bilirubin levels are elevated between days 3 and 5 of life, peaking on day 4 or 5. Within those days, if the bilirubin levels stay moderately low and your baby doesn't have any other medical conditions, the jaundice is not considered harmful. Just keep feeding him, and he'll keep pooping it out. If bilirubin levels are significantly elevated or you baby has other risk factors (like prematurity), the jaundice may need to be treated with phototherapy.

What is phototherapy? This is a special blue light therapy. When these special lights are shined on the baby's skin, it helps the bilirubin move into the gut to be pooped out faster. Phototherapy is ordered by your baby's doctor and might be done in your home. If the bilirubin level is very high, your pediatrician may want to have your baby treated with a larger set of lights at the hospital. The bilirubin blood level is checked repeatedly while your baby is undergoing phototherapy until he has reached and maintained a normal level for his age and risk factors.

If our pediatrician advises me to supplement with formula or completely stop breastfeeding for a time and offer formula instead, how do I protect myself from painful breast engorgement and loss of milk supply? Interrupting breast milk feedings for even one day requires effective breast drainage at least 8 times every 24 hours with a high-quality breast pump. See **Right Pump for You** page 40 and **Combination Feeding Option** page 36. If you do not drain your breasts 8 or more times every 24 hours, you are at increased risk for severe engorgement, plugged milk ducts, breast infection, and a decrease in milk supply. In addition, if your baby needs some time to transition back to full breastfeeding (see **Going Back to the Breast** page 51), you will need to continue pumping. If you develop symptoms of infection (fever, chills, aches, breast pain), see your obstetrician or another healthcare provider as soon as possible and refer to **Plugged Ducts and Mastitis** page 56.

Jaundice is temporary. The changes to your feeding plan will be short term. Stay in touch with your IBCLC until jaundice is resolved and breastfeeding is going smoothly.

References

1. Wilson-Clay B, Hoover K. *The Breastfeeding Atlas* 2017: 14.
2. Reece-Stremtan S, et al. *Breastfeeding Medicine*. Nov 2017;12(9):500-506.
3. Gourley, G, et al. A controlled, randomized, double-blind trial of prophylaxis against jaundice among breastfed newborns. *Pediatrics* 2005 Aug: 116 (2):385-91.
4. Kreamer, et al. A Novel Inhibitor of B-Glucuronidase: L-aspartic Acid. *Pediatric Research* 2001 Nov: 460-464.
5. Gourley, G, et al. The effect of diet on feces and jaundice during the first 3 weeks of life. *Gastroenterology* 1992;103:660-667.
6. Gourley G, et al. Neonatal jaundice and diet. *Arch Pediatr Adolesc Med* 1999;153:184-188.
7. Gourley, G, et al. Inhibition of B-glucuronidase by casein hydrolysate formula. *J Pediatr Gastroenterol Nutr* 1997;25:267-272.
8. Flaherman V, et al. *Breastfeeding Medicine*. 2017;12(5):250-257.

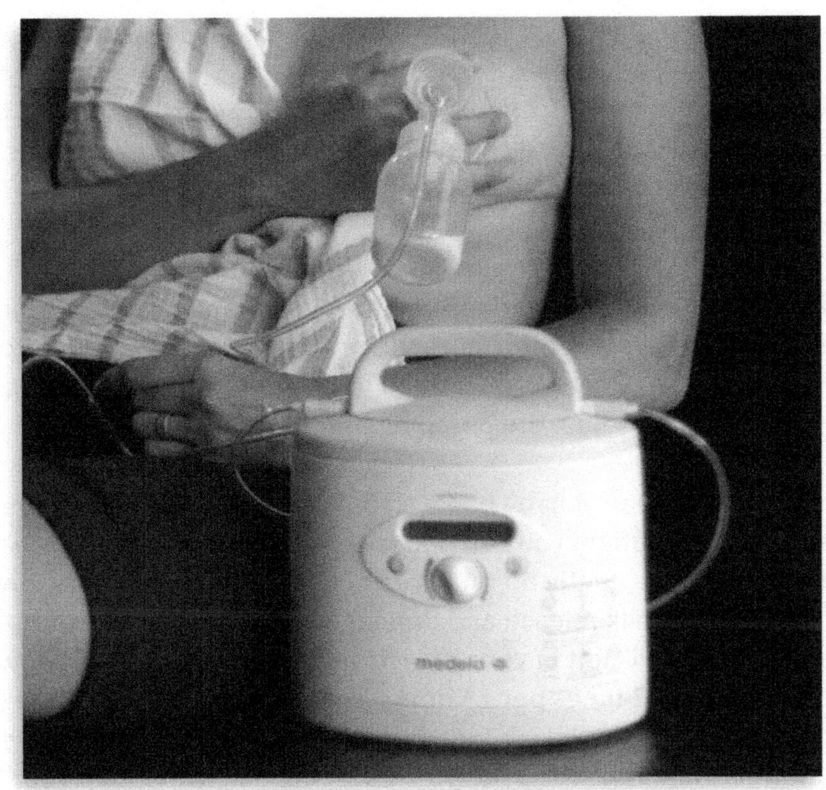

Nipple Shield Use

Short term aid for significant nipple pain or infant's inability to nurse well-- YET

- Using a nipple shield can be very helpful in certain breastfeeding situations involving pain or difficulty latching.[1] In fact, research shows that mothers with premature babies experiencing breastfeeding challenges were able to breastfeed longer than those who were struggling and did not use a shield.[2] However, they are not without risk. Nipple shield use **requires careful follow up and assessment** of mother's milk supply and infant's weight gain. If a nipple shield is necessary for you and your baby, there is a reason. An IBCLC can help you identify the reason and work with you to resolve it.

- Nipple shields come in several sizes and are available at retail stores and online. The size of a nipple shield is unrelated to the size of a breast shield, which is the flange piece used with your pump. **Nipple shields should be fitted to the baby's mouth as well as the mother's nipple**. You may need to experiment to find the best size. If you're not experiencing pain and baby is sucking and gulping, these are indicators of a good fit. If your baby was born less than 38 weeks gestation or weighs less than 7 pounds, you may want to start with a 16 mm shield. Otherwise, start with a 20 mm. Follow the instructions on the package insert for proper usage and cleaning of the shield. There are tricks to help keep them in place.

- Pump milk from your breasts **after every** feeding during which you used the nipple shield. This is necessary to ensure complete breast drainage, which is essential for establishing a full milk supply. See **Protect Your Milk Supply** on page 76 and **Right Pump for You on** page 40.

- If you heard gulping during the feeding, you may only need to pump 5 min on each side for 10 total minutes. Gently compress each breast with your free hand to help the milk release more effectively. Pump long enough to ensure both breasts are soft. As you learn your body, you can adjust the pumping minutes.

- If you didn't hear gulping or if baby had a sleepy feeding, you should pump as if the baby didn't nurse. In this situation, you can pump about 10 minutes on each side for 20 total minutes. Hold the flange gently on one breast while compressing that breast with your free hand, again to aid milk release and drainage. Drained, soft breasts tell your body to keep producing milk. Milk left in your breasts tells your body to slow down production. Draining the breasts 8-12 times per 24 hours is vital during the first 2 weeks of breastfeeding (see pages 76-78). Drained breasts also protect against breast infection (see **Plugged Ducts and Mastitis** page 56). Pumping helps maintain your supply for your baby until you're able to nurse without difficulty.

- Offer your pumped breast milk to your baby if instructed to do so or if you sense the milk is needed. For example, if baby is not pooping 4 or more times per day or if baby doesn't seem relaxed after nursing, offer more milk. See also **Combination Feeding Option** page 36.

- Most babies need nipple shields very temporarily and can come off the shield within 2-3 weeks, sometimes much sooner.[2] Schedule office visits to weigh your baby at least once each week until you are able to nurse without the nipple shield.[3] Using a special scale, your IBCLC can assess how much milk the baby is taking from you while nursing. That information helps you make nursing and pumping decisions until your baby is able to return to full direct breastfeeding. See **Going Back to the Breast** page 51.

Reference

1. Hanna S, Wilson M, Norwood S. A description of breastfeeding outcomes among US mothers using nipple shields. *Midwifery* 2013;29(6):616-621.
2. Meier P, et al. Nipple Shields for Preterm Infants: Effect on Milk Transfer and Duration of Breastfeeding. *Journal of Human Lactation* 2000;16(2):106-114.
3. Wilson-Clay B, Hoover K. *The Breastfeeding Atlas* 2017: 52.

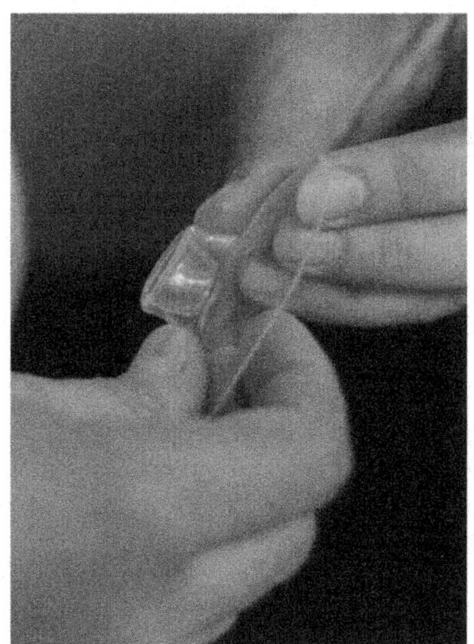

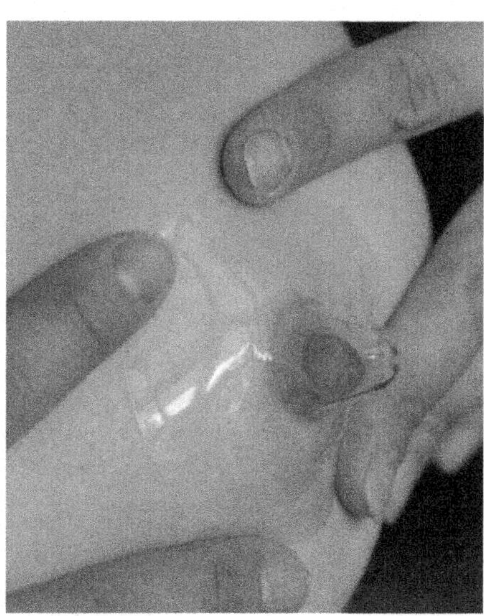

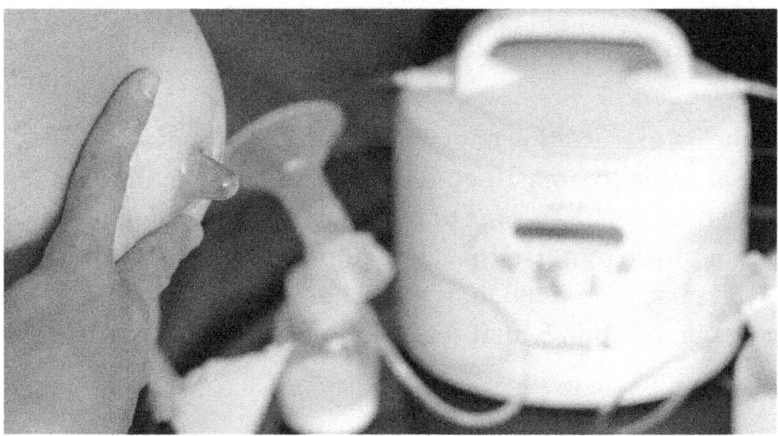

Combination Feeding Option

When your baby isn't ready to do the work of bringing your milk in and keeping your milk in, you find yourself in a situation that requires **you** do a lot of work. You can probably manage all 3 steps, sometimes referred to as "triple feeding", if you have at least one other person who can help you. Trying to triple feed by yourself can put your long-term goals at risk, simply by exhausting you. Designing your short term feeding routine depends upon the time of day and how much help you have.

Remember that prioritizing your pumping rather than your nursing until the baby is nursing effectively protects your milk supply and future success. No matter the situation for each feeding time, don't skip the pumping part! Until the baby is able to do the work, the pump must do the work.

Remember: More pumping now = more nursing later.

So, until you're ready for primetime, nurse for fun and pump for food!

Daytime feeding routine - 45 minutes maximum total time

Daytime Feeding Routine

1. If you are experiencing excruciating pain when your baby nurses, you have the option to skip to # 3. If you are able to breastfeed comfortably, offer the breast and nurse as long as the baby is actively nursing, up to a maximum **total** time of 15 minutes, both breasts combined. You don't have to nurse the same number of minutes on each side because one breast almost always has more milk than the other. If he is not able to become alert enough to actively nurse within 5 minutes, skip to # 3. Note: If a nipple shield is needed for

successful latching, pumping after each nursing is also needed to ensure full establishment and maintenance of supply. See **Nipple Shield Use** page 34.

2. Active nursing involves the baby sucking and swallowing without long pauses in-between or "falling asleep at breast". Active nursing should help your breasts feel softer than before you started nursing. It will be easier to tell the difference when your mature milk arrives. Gently compressing the breast while he nurses can help him get more milk with less effort. Allow him to soften (drain) the first breast before switching to the other to encourage hind milk (higher fat content) intake. How long it takes your baby to "drain" one breast will depend upon the fullness of the breast and his level of alertness at that particular feeding. After the first 48 hours, do NOT use "minutes" as your indication for when to switch breasts or when to determine that the breasts are drained. Monitor how your breasts feel, how he's behaving at each feeding, and how many pees and poops he has every 24 hours. **Watch each other, not the clock**. Note: After the calibration phase, you can work toward a flexible routine if you wish. Establishing a feeding routine prior to 3 weeks of age (the calibration phase) risks your long-term milk supply and possibly your baby's growth. See **Milk Journals** page 97.

3. After baby nurses, have someone else offer the baby his extra milk while you pump. Give him whatever extra milk you have available at that moment. If there is no expressed breast milk available or not enough breast milk to satisfy the baby, go ahead and offer additional formula. Give whatever volume is needed to relax him-- or the specific volume your pediatrician advises. Your helper can also burp the baby and diaper him while you are pumping.

4. If you don't have another person to help you with the feeding, you may need to limit nursing to only 5 minutes so that you can immediately offer extra milk and still have enough time and energy to pump. Remember this is a short-term plan; you're just protecting your milk supply until he is able to nurse better. One father helping his wife adjust to this feeding plan said, "It's ok right now to nurse just for a couple of minutes to **remind him where home is**." If you are on your own for a feeding, after feeding the baby his extra milk, immediately place him in an infant seat or on a blanket beside you for tummy time while you pump. If you get up to diaper him and try to settle him before getting back to pumping, it will be difficult to get back to it. Also, if you are spreading out the feedings and pumpings , you may feel like you are either feeding him or pumping all the time-- and basically you are. Cluster the tasks, even if you have to pump fewer minutes, so that you are able to rest between feeding times. Protecting your rest and minimizing your physical and emotional stress will do more to protect your supply than trying to nurse or pump every hour.

5. Try to pump at least 10 minutes one breast at a time for a total of 20 minutes until you are more comfortable with the process of pumping. "Single pumping" allows you to hold the flange/breast shield against your breast without pressing it in too much, which can block the milk ducts and slow the release of your milk. This also allows you a free hand to gently compress the breast to increase the volume of milk released and decrease the time it takes

to drain the breast. See **Pumping Tips** page 89. Avoid hands-free pumping bras until you've had the opportunity to learn hand expression and hands-on-pumping.

6. When you become more comfortable with the process of pumping and your breasts are releasing milk well, you can try pumping both breasts at the same time (double pumping). You can double pump for 10 minutes. Then switch to single pumping for 5 minutes on each breast, massaging with your free hand while you hold the pump flange to your breast with the other. 10 minutes of double pumping plus 5 minutes on each side single pumping still adds up to 20 minutes total time. After you fully establish your milk supply (30 or more ounces per 24 hours), you will be able to pump fewer minutes.

7. **Pumping should not hurt**. Many mothers have found that applying food grade coconut or olive oil to the nipples prior to pumping increases their comfort. If you are experiencing pain, see **Proper Breast Flange Fit** page 88 and read about how to choose the right breast shield size for you. If the size is too small, your nipple is crowded in the shield and milk cannot release well. If the size is too large, your breast is being pulled down into the shield and milk cannot release well. Also read about how to regulate the suction on your pump. **If you are in pain while pumping, you risk not draining the breasts which could lead to painful engorgement or infection for you and limited milk for baby**. If you're not able to identify what the problem is, make an appointment with your IBCLC for her to observe a pumping session. This can be just as important as her watching a feeding at the breast.

8. While you get something to eat or drink, have someone else clean, according to the manufacturer's instructions, the pump parts that have come into contact with mom's skin or the milk. Then cuddle with the baby or rest until the next feeding in a dark, quiet area. See **Days and Nights Mixed Up** page 28.

9. **In the case of significant pain or exhaustion, it is ok to pump instead of nurse until these problems are resolved**. If you are replacing your baby at the breast for feedings, a rental breast pump is strongly recommended. Again, prioritize protecting milk supply over the direct breastfeeding relationship until baby is ready for primetime.

Nighttime feeding option - 30 minutes maximum total time

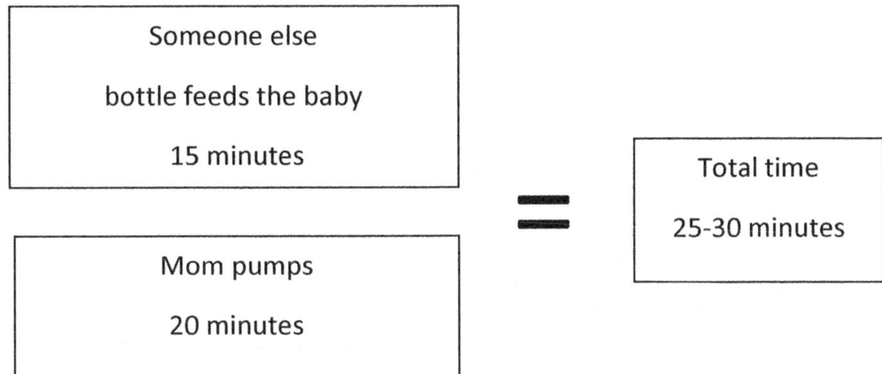

Nighttime feeding routine

1. Offer the breast if the baby has awakened on his own, is alert for the feeding, and is not hurting you while nursing. Nurse for a maximum total time of 10 minutes, both breasts combined, for the middle of the night nursing. After nursing, someone else offers the baby his extra milk, burps him, diapers him, and settles him back to sleep while you pump.

2. Pump for 10-20 minutes at night, depending on how long you did or did not nurse. Pump fewer minutes if he nursed well, more if he didn't. Aim for a 30 minute total feeding/pumping time to maximize your rest, which will maximize your healing and your sense of well-being for the next feeding and the next day.

3. Remember that, as soon as your baby is nursing well, you will be able to just nurse and skip the pumping and the bottles. **Better days...and nights...are coming**.

4. For those moms who will be pumping for more than just a few nights, an investment in an extra set of pump accessories is wise. It's helpful not to have to wash parts in the middle of the night. Plus, if you will be returning to work during your breastfeeding months, you'll appreciate having two sets then for certain.

5. During the night, you can skip the feeding from the breast altogether if you are exhausted and overwhelmed during these hours. Pump for 10-20 minutes and go back to bed while someone else feeds the baby his extra milk, burps, diapers, and settles him back to sleep. (See diagram above.)

The above routines are your game plan until your little one is ready for primetime. When he is gaining weight well, no longer jaundiced, and you are feeling well (any nipple trauma has resolved and any breast engorgement is under control), you can begin the transition back to full breast feeding as you wish. See **Going Back to the Breast** page 51.

The Right Pump for You

I might need to rent a hospital grade breast pump if

- my baby won't wake up to nurse as often as he should.
- I'm dreading feedings because it hurts so much.
- I can tell that my milk is in, but I can't get it out.
- they told me I needed to supplement with formula.
- my baby is in a special care or intensive care nursery.
- I have medical conditions (see **Challenges** page 63).

If you just need occasional milk removal from your breasts for comfort and you already have an established milk supply, a manual breast pump can be ideal and affordable. But if you are experiencing multiple breastfeeding challenges, a key to conquering them is to obtain a breast pump that can drain your breasts well until your baby is able to nurse effectively. Protecting your milk supply is vital for protecting your long-term breastfeeding relationship. See **The Priorities** starting on page 69 for more information.

<u>THE ONLY THING WE CAN'T FIX LATER IS YOUR MILK SUPPLY</u>

A high-quality breast pump, like a multiple-user rental pump, ***buys you time.*** *Remember! The* ***most important*** *step toward long-term success is a* ***short-term*** *focus on establishing and protecting your milk supply. So, if the baby isn't able to do the work of breastfeeding yet or your body isn't responding to the baby's signals yet, the hospital grade rental pump can do the work.*

What is a multiple-user rental breast pump?

Typically, a multiple-user or "hospital grade" breast pump is a large electric breast pump that is available in hospitals and in the community as a rental item. The FDA does not use the term "hospital grade" in its classification system. It describes breast pumps simply as "single-user" and "multiple-user".[1] Until there is an industry quality standard for breast pumps, consult with your IBCLC regarding your options and ask her to make a recommendation based upon your individual situation.[2] Research does not tell us which type of pump is best for most moms because moms are highly individual and research studies are non-standardized, so it is nearly impossible to control for all variables.[3]

Multiple-user rental breast pumps are NOT

Not available for purchase in retail stores or consignment shops. Multiple-user rental pumps (i.e. Medela Symphony™) are valued at least $2000. Most families typically do not purchase them, but instead rent them for $75-$125 a month. Rental pumps are designed to replace the work of the baby at the breast until the baby is ready to do the work. They can also sustain milk supply long term for a mom who prefers to pump her milk for baby.

Not the type of pump your insurance company will provide you. A manual breast pump (i.e. Medela Harmony™ or Avent Comfort™) or a small motor, single-user breast pump that is designed for occasional use (i.e. Medela PumpInStyle™ or Ameda Purely Yours™) can be helpful when your milk supply is established and your baby is able to nurse effectively. If your insurance company provides you with one of these pumps, hold on to it. Many moms are able to "graduate" to a non-rental pump after both their milk supply and their baby are ready for primetime. Many moms report that their manual pumps are more comfortable and effective for occasional use than their single-user electric pumps are. You can see what works best for you. Consult with your IBCLC to make sure you are on track to meet your individual goals.

Not the type of pump that increases your risk for infection. Multiple-user rental pumps typically have three to five-year warranty and require a separate accessory kit. They are designed to be used by multiple mothers. In addition to having separate accessories, there is a filter that prevents another woman's viruses, bacteria, and funguses from infecting you via the pump. Single-user breast pumps should not be shared, **even if you purchase new tubing and parts** that touch mom and milk.[1] This means purchasing them **at garage sales or consignment stores is a health risk**. If it was effective and safe to share single-user pumps, hospitals would use these cheaper pumps for their patients to use while in the hospital. No matter how budget- conscious a hospital is, they do not use small motor, single-user breast pumps. The FDA encourages mothers to report any injuries to them at 1-800-FDA-1088.

Multiple-user rental pumps are important because

Establishing your full milk supply is essentially the only thing that can't be done later. One researcher describes establishing milk supply as "One event that is either achieved or not achieved".[4,5] The "Calibration Phase" window for establishing your milk supply is the first three weeks, with the most important days being the first five.[6-11] If you are already past the three-week window, don't worry – it's not too late to maximize your supply as much as possible. Consult with your IBCLC as soon as possible for additional strategies to increase your milk supply. Excellent information about increasing milk supply is also found in Diana West and Lisa Marasco's book, *Making More Milk*.[25]

Experts agree that, when there are breastfeeding difficulties, pumping with a high-quality breast pump early and often is the key to establishing a full long-term supply.[6-20] The question is: Can your pump drain your breasts? As far as how long you need to pump, most clinicians recommend at least 15 minutes per pumping session. Your total 24-hour milk production goal is at least 26 ounces. If you are doing some nursing and some pumping, you obviously won't know what your 24-hour total production is, but you can look at your baby's intake from a bottle and get a pretty good idea. For example, when your baby no longer needs formula supplement, your supply is clearly increasing. See **Milk Journals** page 97.

A 24-hour milk production of 28-35 ounces is considered a fully established supply, which sets you up for long-term success (see **Protecting Your Milk Supply** page 76). After the calibration phase, you should be able to gradually decrease the number of minutes per pumping and eventually decrease the number of pumping sessions per day without harming your milk supply.[21,4] Note: After the calibration phase, over-pumping, which can result in over-production of breastmilk, is not helpful and might actually decrease the nutrient value of your milk.[3] Unless you have a 2-pound preemie who will eventually need all of it, having a "freezer full of breastmilk" is not necessarily a good thing.

The Academy of Breastfeeding Medicine recommends that if your "**baby is not gaining weight normally or supplementation is being used** because of low milk production, during the initiation or maintenance of milk supply",[22] effective and frequent milk removal from the breasts is required. For "women with babies who are ineffective at milk removal or unable to feed at the breast", they advise hand expression of colostrum in addition to pumping with a "**hospital grade** (multiple-user rental) **pump using hands-on technique** at maximum comfort vacuum".[22] See **Pumping Tips** on page 89.

Replacing your baby at the breast requires a pump that mimics the baby as much as possible.[23] You can express milk with your hands if you just feel a little uncomfortable after your baby breastfeeds or after you pump. But if you are replacing your baby at the breast by hand-expressing, you are risking your supply. A recent study showed that mothers who exclusively hand expressed their milk for 7 days produced about half as much milk as mothers who expressed their milk with an electric breast pump. And even after switching to an electric pump after day 7, their production did not increase.[24]

All breast pumps are not created equal. There are aspects of suction level and cycle pattern that are important to comfort, speed, and effectiveness of different pumps.[23,25] Manual pumps can be comfortable, effective, and affordable for moms who already have an established supply.[3,25] But in general terms, when it comes to single-user electric breast pumps, you get what you pay for. West and Marasco explain in *Making More Milk*, "Cheaper pumps wear out quickly and don't draw milk as efficiently...Mothers almost universally find that they are able to extract milk more easily and quickly with the hospital-grade (multiple-user rental) pumps than with even the best consumer-grade (single-user) pumps."[25]

Use caution when comparing online reviews. Keep in mind that internet reviews are written by women of very different situations. For example, every woman has a different amount of glandular tissue (the part of the breast that produces milk). That glandular tissue then produces and stores an amount of milk that is unique to each mother, called "storage capacity". Each mother has her own storage capacity. In addition, her production amount can vary from day to day and within each day.[20] So, if a mom who has a 10-ounce storage capacity (see **The Challenges** section page 63) is reviewing an inexpensive single-user pump, she may have a good outcome with that pump because her naturally high milk volume is not dependent upon complete breast drainage. However, if a mother with a 4-ounce storage capacity reviewed the same pump, she might report that it did not fully drain her and, as a result, she didn't have enough milk for her baby in the long run.

If you're going to do the work of pumping, make sure your pump can do the work. It is the drained breast that tells your brain to make more milk. The partially drained breast tells your brain that not all the milk is needed and reduces the production accordingly.[9] That means that you can be working hard by pumping 8 or more times daily and still not reach your goals *simply because the pump isn't working as hard as you are.*

Your comfort matters. A lot. Excellent studies have shown that listening to music, warming your breasts prior to pumping, using warm breast shields, and massaging your breasts during pumping increases the amount of milk you can express.[3,26-28] It's also important to know that increasing the suction beyond what is comfortable for you risks traumatizing your nipples and will not increase your milk supply. The opposite is true. Your milk will come out faster and there will be more of it when you turn up the suction level only to the highest level within your comfort.

Affording a rental breast pump

If your family truly cannot afford the rental fee, purchasing a high quality manual breast pump can be a more effective way to express your milk than a small motor electric pump.[3,25,30] Something else to keep in mind is that some rental stations will agree to rent in 2 week increments or offer assistance programs. If you are WIC eligible, check with your county's office.

To help put the cost into perspective, a $75 monthly rental fee seems like a large investment until it is compared with the consequences of not establishing a full milk supply during the Calibration Phase.[25] Long-term formula supplementation and the healthcare expenditures associated with complete weaning from the protection of mother's milk are far more costly. *Many families find that they **only need the rental pump for the first month** because problems can be overcome and full breastfeeding can be resumed even before the first month rental is up.* So, the investment is totally worth it. And, grandparents, consider this: the baby will never know if you bought him cute clothes or fun toys during his first month of life. **Perhaps giving that one month rental as a gift would be a cool idea.**

References

1. Food and Drug Administration (US FDA). Medical Devices: Breastpumps. www.fda.gov/medicaldevices . Updated August 24, 2016. Accessed February 2018.
2. Flaherman VJ, Lee H. "Breastfeeding" by Feeding Expressed Mother's Milk. *Pediatr Clin North Am*. 2013 Feb;60(1):227-246.
3. Becker GE, Smith HA, Cooney F. Methods of milk expression for lactating women. *Cochrane Database of Systematic Reviews*. 2016, 9:CD006170.
4. Mohrbacher, N; Kendall-Tackett, K. *Breastfeeding Made Simple* 2010; 110-111, 295.
5. Neville, MC, et al. Lactogenesis. The transition from pregnancy to lactation. *Pediatric Clinics of North America* 2001;48:35-52.
6. Ramsay D, et al. Milk flow rates can be used to identify and investigate milk ejection in women expressing breast milk using an electric breast pump. *Breastfeeding Medicine* 2006;1(1):14-23.
7. Slusher T, Slusher IL, Biomdo M, et al. Electric breast pump use increases maternal milk volume in African nurseries. *Journal of Tropical Pediatrics* 2007;53(2):125-130.
8. Meier P, Patel A, Hoban R, et al. Which breast pump for which mother: an evidence based approach to individualizing breast pump technology. *Journal of Perinatology* 2016;36(7):493-499.
9. Mohrbacher, N. *Breastfeeding Answers Made Simple* 2010; 467-469.
10. Parker LA, et al. Effect of early breast milk expression on milk volume and timing of lactogenesis stage II among mothers of very low birth weight infants: a pilot study. *Journal of Perinatology* 2012;32(2):205-209.
11. Parker L, Sullivan S, Kreuger C, et al. Association of timing of initiation of breastmilk expression on milk volume and timing of lactogenesis stage II among mothers of very low birth-weight infants. *Breastfeeding Medicine* 2015;10(2):84-91.
12. Hill, et al. Effects of pumping style on milk production in mothers of non-nursing preterm infants. *Journal of Human* Lactation 1999;15:209-215.
13. Hill P, Aldag J, Chatterton R, et al. Comparison of milk output between mothers of preterm and term infants: the first 6 weeks after birth. *Journal of Human Lactation* 2005;21(1):22-30.
14. Hill PD, Aldag JC. Predictors of term infant feeding at week 12 postpartum. *Journal of Perinatal and Neonatal Nursing* 2007;21(3):250-255.
15. Brownell E, Howard CR, Lawrence RA, et al. Delayed onset of lactogenesis II predicts the cessation of any or exclusive breastfeeding. *Journal of Pediatrics 2012;7(6):489-509.*
16. Meier, P, et al. Supporting breastfeeding in the neonatal intensive care unit. *Pediatric Clinics of North America* 2013:60(1), 209-226.
17. Meier P, Furman L, Degenhardt M. Increased lactation for late preterm infants and mothers: Evidence and management strategies to protect breastfeeding. *Journal of Midwifery and Women's Health* 2007;52:579-587.
18. Meier, P, et al (2004). The Rush mothers' club: breastfeeding interventions for mothers of very low birth weight infants. *Journal of Obstetric, Gynecologic and Neonatal Nursing* 2004;33:164-174.
19. Morton J, et al. Combining hand techniques with electric pumping increases milk production in mothers of preterm infants. *Journal of Perinatology* 2009;(29)11:757-764.
20. Kent J. Volume and frequency of Breastfeedings and Fat Content of Breast Milk Throughout the Day. *Pediatrics* 2006;*117(3).*
21. Prime D, Kent J, Hepworth A, Trengrove N, Hartmann P. Dynamics of milk removal during simultaneous breast expression in women. *Breastfeeding Medicine*. 2012 April;7(2):100-6.
22. Reece-Stremtan S, et al. *Breastfeeding Medicine*. Nov 2017;12(9):500-506.
23. Meier, P, et al (2016). Which Breast Pump for Which Mother: An Evidence-Based Approach to Individualizing Breast Pump Technology. *J Perinatology* 2016.
24. Lussier M, Brownell E, Proulx T, et al. Daily breastmilk volume in mothers of very low birthweight neonates: a repeated-measures randomized trial of hand expression versus electric pump expression. *Breastfeeding Medicine* 2015;10(6):312-317.
25. West D, Marasco L. *Making More Milk* 2009: 158-160.
26. Jones E, Dimmock P, Spencer S. A randomised controlled trial to compare methods of milk expression after preterm delivery. *Arch Dis Child Fetal Neonatal Ed*. 2001 Sep;85(2):F91-5.
27. Yigit F, Cigdem Z, Temizsoy E, Cingi M, Korel O, Yildirim E, Ovali F. Does warming the breasts affect the amount of milk production? *Breastfeeding Medicine*. 2012 Dec;7(6):487-8.
28. Kent J, Geddes D, Hepworth A, Hartmann P. Effect of warm breastshields on breast milk pumping. *Journal of Human Lactation*. 2011 Nov;27(4):331-8.
29. Kent JC, Mitoulas LR, Cregan MD, Geddes DT, Larsson M, Doherty DA, Hartmann PE. Importance of vacuum for milk expression. *Breastfeeding Medicine* 2008 Mar;3(1):11-19.
30. Fewtrell M, Lucas P, Collier S, Singhal A, Ahlowalia J, Lucas A. Randomized trial comparing the efficacy of a novel manual breast pump with a standard electric breast pump in mothers who delivered preterm infants. *Pediatrics* 2001 Jun;107(6):1291-7.

Bottles, Pacifiers, and Formula

Bottles, pacifiers, and formula are currently considered problems in the ideal world but considered solutions in the real world. What's most important is that you need information about bottles, pacifiers, and infant formula that **protects your breastfeeding relationship** as much as possible. Mothers who have medical risk factors may need to use supplemental nutrition long term, even if they have received the right help at the right time and followed the right plan of care for success (see **Challenges** page 63). That may not be your situation, and short term supplementation is all you will need. Either way, it....is....ok. Research tells us that high levels of the stress hormone, cortisol, can delay your milk coming in.[1] So, relaxing about the need for a change in your plan of care may actually help you milk come in sooner!

Pacifiers

Are pacifiers ok to use in the first week?

In the first couple of days, when your milk *content* is fantastic, but your milk *volume* is naturally limited, your baby may want to "non-nutritively" or "pacifier" suck for comfort. You can respond to this by allowing him to remain at the breast, offer a clean finger to suck, or offer a pacifier. If you have significant nipple pain or damage to the skin on your nipples, you may want to avoid comfort nursing until healed. Also have an IBCLC assess your baby's mouth and your positioning and latch as soon as possible. See **Nipple Pain** page 24.

Why am I being told not to give my baby a pacifier?

Some babies cannot remember how to latch well to the breast after having sucked on a rigid artificial nipple. *Some* mothers offer a pacifier when their baby should be nursing. Also, not *every* mother has access to an IBCLC who can provide timely help that may be needed for the babies who are struggling with latch. You are also advised not to give your baby a pacifier because current recommendations are largely based upon non-current research.

What does the research say about pacifiers?

The Academy of Breastfeeding Medicine explains that research from over a decade ago may not have isolated the many variables that are involved in the relationship between breastfeeding, pacifier use, and supplementation.[2] So, after examining more current evidence, they have concluded:

"Some earlier research showed that pacifier use in the neonatal period was detrimental to exclusive and overall breastfeeding. A recent (literature) review found that **pacifier use in healthy term breastfeeding infants, started at birth or after lactation was established, did not significantly affect the prevalence or duration of exclusive and partial breastfeeding up to 4 months of age**".[3]

"Many breastfeeding advocates have negative views of pacifiers. However, the '**highest level of evidence does not support an adverse effect of pacifier use on breastfeeding** duration or exclusivity'".[4]

"Associations between shortened duration of breastfeeding reported in some observational studies probably reflect numerous complex issues related to breastfeeding difficulties, or intention to wean".[5]

What are the consequences of *over-using* a pacifier in the early days of breastfeeding?
You risk underfeeding your baby and you risk not establishing your milk supply if you use a pacifier inappropriately. Examples of inappropriate use would be:

- You let your baby suck on a pacifier instead of nurse because you have visitors or because you're trying to feed on a schedule.
- It's been an hour since he nursed last and you use the paci to "hold him off".
- You put the paci in his mouth every time he whimpers.

Does every baby who is offered an artificial nipple experience nipple confusion?
No. Many can go back and forth easily. However, even if your baby can do both, it is important that you listen to your baby and learn his different cries. His cries will differ for things like hunger, pain, diaper discomfort, and sleepiness.

Does using a pacifier automatically destroy my goal of exclusive breastfeeding?
Absolutely not. The only way to truly destroy your breastfeeding goals is to stop draining your breasts. Just make sure the pacifier isn't keeping your baby from draining your breasts 8 or more times every 24 hours.

Is using a pacifier in the first two days of life going to automatically cause my baby to lose an excessive amount of weight?
No. A very well-designed research study done in 2010 found that excessive neonatal weight loss in the first few days of age can be related to the amount of IV fluids the mother received in labor.[6] This is an especially important consideration for first time mothers who typically have longer labors and epidural anesthesia, both of which increase her exposure to IV fluid.

The same study found that excessive weight loss in the first few days is NOT related to pacifier use. The data regarding maternal fluid weight gained during labor affecting infant fluid weight lost after birth was statistically significant; the data regarding pacifier use was not. Those findings are clinically significant given the amount of parent concerns about this issue. The data shows that the **pacifier babies in this study actually lost less weight than the non-pacifier babies.**[6]

Does the type of pacifier matter?
Yes, for some babies. The type of pacifier may affect your baby's ability to transition back and forth from breast to bottle. Pacifiers that have a slanted (orthodontic) nipple or have a nipple that is pinched at the base don't feel like a mother's nipple. These types of pacifiers also require your baby to clench his mouth shut in order to keep the paci in his mouth. Choose a pacifier that has a uniform shaped nipple and encourages him to keep his jaw down and tongue over his bottom gum.

Note: If your baby refuses all pacifiers except the orthodontic shape, have his tongue evaluated. Some babies who are tongue-tied can keep this pacifier in place better because they hold it in their mouths by clenching the jaw shut and pushing the tongue up on the nipple.

Which pacifier should we purchase if we want to use one?
One pacifier that is designed to keep the jaw down and tongue out is the *Soothie™*. It is a large, round pacifier made of soft silicone.

What are the alternatives to using a pacifier?
Some mothers prefer to have all of the baby's sucking needs met by the breast. This is fine, but if you do not prefer this approach, you or another caregiver may offer a clean finger for the baby to suck on. Just like when you use a pacifier, be sure not to artificially lengthen the time between his feedings at the breast. In addition, observe your baby's ability to latch on well to the breast following finger sucking.

What if my baby has taken an artificial nipple (pacifier or bottle) and now refuses to latch to the breast for feedings?
If your baby temporarily is confused, hang in there with him. You can help him remember what to do. Refer to **Going Back to the Breast** on page 51 for specific suggestions. In the meantime, you could try a nipple shield, which will make your nipple feel like a bottle nipple and serve as "training wheels" back to the breast. See **Nipple Shield Use** page 34 for important information on safe and effective usage. You can express your milk and feed it in bottles until you're able to work with an IBCLC for help with the transition. Read about how to protect your milk supply in the meantime in the **Combination Feeding Option** on page 36.

Bottles

Which bottle is best when breastfeeding?
*During early breastfeeding, the author's best experience has been with a standard bottle and a **rubber nipple**.*

Why am I being told not to give my baby a bottle?
Some babies have difficulty latching to the breast after having sucked from a bottle with a more rigid nipple and immediate flow of milk. *Some* mothers offer their babies additional milk (either expressed breast milk or infant formula) from a bottle and do not ensure that their breasts are drained. This can prevent you from establishing your individual maximum milk supply.

Will giving my baby a bottle in the short-term harm my long-term breastfeeding goals?
Not if you protect your milk supply. If you are protecting your supply, bottles can actually save breastfeeding (see **Combination Feeding Option** page 36). While there are alternative methods for feeding extra milk (see page 72 in the **Priorities** section), offering your breast milk in a bottle might be needed in the first week of life. If your baby loses more than 8% of his birth weight, this could indicate a problem with the way he is feeding or your milk availability.[7] If you haven't yet met with a hospital IBCLC, ask for one to come and to assess you and your baby. About 19% of babies born to first time mothers lose more than 10% of their body weight, most requiring supplemental nutrition.[6] That means about **1 out of every 5 babies will need extra milk during the first week**. Expressing your own milk should always be the first thing to do, but it may not be sufficient volume for the first several days. Unless there is safe donor breast milk available, the supplemental nutrition will be infant formula.

Important!
The need for formula (Priority #1) = the need for pumping (Priorities #2 & #3).
Formula = Pumping

Make sure to drain your breasts with the highest quality breast pump you can afford for *at least as many times* as the baby takes a bottle of either your milk or infant formula.[7] Offer only as much formula as your pediatrician orders.

See **Right Pump for You** page 40 and **Priorities** page 49 for more information regarding formula and protecting your milk supply until the baby is ready for primetime.

If we need a bottle, does it matter what kind of bottle we use?
It matters for some babies. If you are struggling to find a bottle your baby will take without problems, consult your IBCLC or pediatrician. In general, start with a small rubber nipple that is slow or standard flow and a bottle without any "bells and whistles". Keep it simple. Don't

worry about claims of it feeling like a breast, flowing like a breast, or reducing gas and colic, etc. Just get your milk out of you and into a non-complicated bottle for now.

Can I mix breastmilk and formula in the same bottle?
Yes, but alternating them is better for the baby. Mixing formula into expressed breast milk (EBM) can decrease mineral absorption and increase growth of bacteria.[8] So, at each feeding, it's better to offer all EBM or all formula, even if that means you have to feed the baby 3 feedings of formula in a row until you have pumped enough EBM for a full feeding. That way your baby gets the full benefit of your breastmilk.

Formula

What do experts say about infant formula?
Physicians specializing in Breastfeeding Medicine include the following in their protocol for supplementary feeding of a healthy, full-term newborn:

"Protein hydrosylate formulas are preferable to standard artificial milks as they avoid exposure to cow's milk proteins, reduce bilirubin levels more rapidly, and may convey the psychological message that the supplement is a temporary therapy, not a permanent inclusion of artificial feedings. Supplementation with glucose water is not appropriate."[7]

Will my baby need to continue this type of formula?
If your baby needs formula supplement longer than the first couple of weeks of life, your pediatrician will guide you on the appropriate choice of infant formula. Family history of food allergy should be reported to your pediatrician.

Will my baby prefer formula over my breastmilk?
No! Breastmilk smells and tastes very sweet. Formula smells and tastes like vitamins soaked in canned milk. Which would you prefer?

How do I prepare formula?
Carefully follow the instructions on the label. Do not overheat, but do not offer cool formula. Ask your pediatrician if there are any additional considerations specific to your situation, for example your water source. For more information, you can go to htts://www.fda.gov/Food/ResourcesForYou/HealthEducators/ucm089629.htm.

How much formula do I give my baby?

Your pediatrician will advise you regarding how much extra milk your baby needs. You will need to factor into the equation how well your baby is nursing from the breast and how much expressed breast milk he is receiving. Other factors that guide supplementation volumes are how many pees and poops your baby is having and if he is jaundiced.

The following information is from the Academy of Breastfeeding Medicine supplementation protocol to give you a general idea of "normal expectations" during the first 4 days of your baby's life.[7] Limited colostrum volumes increase to larger transition milk volumes. Again, keep in mind that you may have breastfed or supplemented with some of your milk prior to supplementing with formula.

These are **AVERAGE** milk intake volumes per feeding session and are **guidelines** only. Remember that feeding sessions may be more frequent than every three hours and your baby may need a different volume than listed.

1st 24 hours = 2-10 ml per feeding
24-48 hours = 5-15 ml per feeding
48-72 hours = 15-30 ml per feeding
72-96 hours = 30-60 ml per feeding[7]

After day 4, babies' milk intake per feeding varies widely. Babies will require different volumes based on their weight and mother's milk availability at each feeding. Your pediatrician can guide you further regarding supplementation recommendations for your baby. For information regarding milk supply and supplementation with your milk, see **Right Pump for You** page 40 and **Combination Feeding Option** page 36.

References

1. Dewey, K, et al. Risk Factors for Suboptimal Infant Breastfeeding Behavior, Delayed Onset of Lactation, and Excess Neonatal Weight Loss. *Pediatrics* 2003;112;607-619.
2. Holmes A, McLeod A, and Bunik M. *Breastfeeding Medicine*. December 2013;8(6):469-473.
3. Jaafar, SH, et al. *Cochrane Database Syst Rev* 2016 Aug 30;8:CD007202. Effect of restricted pacifier use in breastfeeding term infants for increasing duration of breastfeeding.
4. O'Connor, NR, et al. Pacifiers and breastfeeding: A systematic review. *Arch Pediatr Adolesc Med* 2009;163;378-382.
5. Wilson-Clay B, Hoover, K. *The Breastfeeding Atlas* 2017;121.
6. Chantry, C, et al. Excess Weight Loss in First-Born Breastfed Newborn Relates to Maternal Intrapartum Fluid Balance. *Pediatrics 2011;127;e171.*
7. Kellams A, Harrel C, Omage S, Gregory C, Rosen-Carole C, and the Academy of Breastfeeding Medicine. *Breastfeeding Medicine*. May 2017,12(4):188-198.
8. Mohrbacher, N. *Breastfeeding Answers Made Simple* 2010; 355.

Going Back to the Breast

You can do it!

Answers to questions about returning to mostly feeding from the breast if your baby has been mostly feeding from bottles

When do we start trying to go back to the breast? One way to think of it is full term + full milk supply = full breastfeeding. However, you don't have to have all the pieces to start putting the puzzle together. Consult yourself, your baby, your pediatrician, and your IBCLC to determine readiness to begin the process of transitioning the baby back to the breast. You may also want to arrange for another adult to help you during the few days of transition. You will benefit greatly from an extra pair of hands, because you may briefly need to do all three feeding steps: nursing, supplementing, and pumping.

How long will it take? When both mother and baby are ready to begin the process of transitioning from mostly feeding expressed breast milk from an alternative feeding device to mostly direct breastfeeding, patience and persistence are the keys to success. Congratulate yourself for maintaining your milk supply up to this point and anticipate the need for continued flexibility. Some babies transition in a day or two. Some take longer. A lot depends on how significant your risk factors were and perhaps still are.

What if it's not happening quickly? Most learning processes are accomplished in stages. Transitioning back to the breast is no exception. The first stage includes time spent skin-to-skin at non-feeding times, bottle feeding skin-to-skin, and opportunities to nuzzle the breast and lick the nipple. The second stage includes nursing from an empty breast after a bottle feeding and nursing with a nipple shield. The third stage is feeding directly from the breast without a nipple shield.

How do we begin? When you are ready to attempt a feeding at the breast, a few tricks may be helpful. Bring your baby in a calm, alert state to your breast. Someone else may need to feed him part of his feeding from the bottle while you pump for just a moment to get your milk started flowing. Then offer the breast. This way, your baby is not frantically hungry (not a good frame of mind for learning) as he approaches the breast. Then he learns that milk comes out of you immediately just like it does from the bottle. If this technique works, continue it for a day or two. Then see if he can begin feeding at the breast without the preliminaries. The **Milk Journals** page 97 can help you track your progress. Take your baby in for a weight check after about a week of feeding mostly from the breast to put your mind at ease about his successful transition.

Can we use a nipple shield? You can think of a nipple shield as "training wheels" back to the breast. Your baby may temporarily require the sensation of the artificial nipple in his mouth. The shield will create a "bottle feeling" in his soft palate, which should help him to begin sucking.

Some preemies breastfeed and gain weight better with a nipple shield.[1] Often their cheeks don't have the fat pads necessary to create enough suction to hold mom's nipple in the mouth for continuous nursing. They become fatigued and appear to be sleepy at the breast. The nipple shield reminds them to suck and helps them maintain suction.[2] A trick some moms use is to pump just until their milk lets-down before applying the shield and attaching the baby so that milk is already flowing with his first suck. This technique can be discontinued as baby learns to feed from the breast. See **Nipple Shield Use** page 34. **Pumping after nursing** with a nipple shield, or "insurance pumping", is **required to maintain your supply** until baby is able to nurse without the shield.

Can we supplement at the breast? You can get extra milk into your baby while you're nursing him by using a nursing supplementer (i.e. Medela SNS). Although it can be complicated to use, the at-the-breast supplementer does have the advantage of providing a flow of milk at the breast to encourage latch and suckling, as well as, eliminating the bottle during the transition back to the breast. It can also replace the bottle for families who will be in long term supplementation situations, for example nursing premature twins. Depending on your situation, "insurance pumping" after nursing with the supplementer may be required to maintain your milk supply. Meet with your IBCLC for more guidance.

What if my baby is super-stubborn? One technique that has been successful for some moms who have especially stubborn babies is to co-bathe. Spending time belly-to-belly together in a warm bath can obviously provide good skin-to-skin time, but it might also reactivate some of the hard-wired early breastfeeding behaviors.[2,3] Also visit Dr. Theresa Nesbitt and Nancy Mohrbacher's website www.naturalbreastfeeding.com to view videos on "Natural Feeding Position". If you continue to struggle, get in touch with your IBCLC and/or other helpers for further assistance.

Is any time of day better than another? For the baby who demands a fast flow, it may help to attempt your first feedings at the breast in the early morning. Most moms typically have more milk available first thing in the morning, which is helpful. The opposite would be the case for the baby who prefers a slower flow. Try the evening feeds first since they typically are lower volume, slower flow. Also, you can bring the baby to the breast just as he begins stirring from sleep. If he's not quite awake, he might be more flexible.

How many feedings a day should we try to do at the breast? Start with one or two feedings per day for a couple of days. Monitor for any nipple pain and continue to "insurance pump". Supporting your milk supply during the transition process continues to be the priority. Pumping briefly is necessary in the first stage of the process. Expressing your milk for 5 minutes or so on each side and gently massaging with your free hand can ensure that, if baby left large volumes of milk in the breast, you're providing a "safety net" for your supply. Pump longer if needed for complete breast drainage in the early days of transition. Track your residual volumes, which is the amount of breast milk you pump out after nursing. Also track the volume of expressed breast milk supplement your baby is taking. You can utilize the **Milk Journals** page 97 for help keeping track of your progress.

What if it still hurts? If you're experiencing pain with latching, continue pumping 8 or more times daily, limit or avoid nursing, and call for an appointment with your IBCLC. Ask her to look at his lips, tongue, and jaw. There may be a physical reason your baby is still struggling to latch. Although it may not resolve all problems, prompt treatment of a tongue-tie can be very helpful.[4-13] You don't have to be able to see a tongue tie for it to cause pain and problems. Ultrasound research shows that even if they were nursing well, tongue-tied infants often compress the nipple and have difficulty sustaining suction.[10]

How do I know if he is making progress? One way of determining if he is nursing effectively is to compare the amount of supplement your baby takes in a bottle after nursing to the amount of supplement he takes at a feeding when he has not nursed. If he takes a much lower volume of supplement after nursing, he is starting to nurse more effectively. Similarly, if your residual pumping volume is much less after he nurses than what it was when you just pumped without nursing, he is starting to nurse more effectively. Nursing effectively can be thought of as alert and rhythmically swallowing while he's nursing, needs little to no supplement from a bottle after nursing, and nursing well enough that you don't have to pump after nursing. Avoid nursing more than twice daily until he displays these signs of readiness to nurse. One way to think of it is: gulping = gaining.

Can I just nurse at night and pump and bottle feed during the day? How you manage day feeds and night feeds depends on several factors as the transition to the breast progresses. You may choose not to attempt feeding from the breast at night until your baby has reached the "nurses effectively" phase. Until he is nursing effectively, you still have to offer a bottle of expressed breast milk after he nurses. Plus, you still have to pump. All three steps at night are a recipe for exhaustion and consequently a premature weaning risk. Evaluate your feeding plan as you go to ensure that it continues to be do-able for you.

How do we know it's time to do more feedings at the breast? When you see consistent progress, you can advance to more feedings at the breast per 24 hours. If your baby is able to nurse effectively for one or two feedings, but not ready yet to nurse effectively at every feeding, you might want to feed directly from the breast for the night feedings only. This will allow for more rest at night. Then you can work toward nursing all day in addition to at night. Take cues from your baby and your body to determine how quickly to increase the number of feedings at the breast without the extra steps of insurance pumping and supplementation.

When can we stop the extra steps of pumping and supplementing? Before discontinuing insurance pumping and supplementation, ensure you have 100% 24-hour milk supply and baby has 100% suckling capabilities for 24 hours of breastfeeding. If at all possible, have a consult with a IBCLC who can assess before and after feeding gram weights to determine the amount of milk transferred during a feeding. Then compare that to what you would typically pump and how much the baby would take *at that particular time of day*. It is important to "compare apples to apples".

What if I haven't been able to produce 100% of what my baby needs? If there is a discrepancy between how much milk you have available per feeding and how much your baby needs per feeding, or if your baby is not able to do all of the work on his own yet, there are options for supplementing at the breast DURING breastfeeding. **Every drop of breast milk counts!** Consult with your IBCLC about the possibility of using a nursing supplementer. Continue seeing your IBCLC regularly during the supplementation phase. You can always nurse and then follow with a bottle long term if you wish.

How will we know things are going well? Normal stooling and sleeping patterns are good indicators of transition success. Then a weight check appointment after you have been fully transitioned to the breast for a week is helpful to put your mind at ease that the transition has been completely successful.

What if it's not working? If you are not able to make the transition quickly, avoid frustrating yourself or your baby. Take a break for several days; then try again. If you have established a full supply, you can maintain your milk supply for the short term or long term with a rental pump. Continue to check in with your IBCLC for more ideas. If your baby is fussy regardless of feeding method, make an appointment with your pediatrician to discuss the several possible causes and treatments.

What if I would rather just keep pumping for bottles? Even though it's more work than just nursing, if you would prefer to maintain your supply long term with a breast pump and continue offering your baby breast milk in a bottle, that is perfectly fine. A risk associated with exclusively feeding any type of milk in bottles is the risk of chronic over-feeding. Because the bottle behaves differently than the breast, babies can take more from a bottle than they would from the breast. But, obviously, getting more breastmilk than he needs is much better than getting more formula than he needs.

Do I need to keep using the hospital grade rental breast pump if I have a full milk supply? Keep in mind that, until your baby is able to nurse effectively at every feeding, a rental pump continues to be the optimal equipment for maintenance of milk production in the short or long term. If you decide to try a single-user small motor retail pump (Medela PumpInStyle™ or Ameda Purely Yours™) after establishing your supply, be aware that these pumps are designed for use 1-2 times per day. Some moms complain of nipple soreness when pumping frequently with the smaller motor. Some moms also report they have to pump more minutes to get the same amount of milk. The most important difference is that a small motor retail pump may not fully drain your breasts which, if happening frequently, signals your brain to slow down production.

Before you return your rental pump, use your small motor pump for a complete week to be sure you are maintaining your supply and that your nipples and breasts don't hurt. After you return your pump, carefully monitor your supply, as well as your baby's behavior and stooling pattern, for several weeks. The decrease of your milk supply can be very slow, but very real. You've worked hard to get where you are. From a simple financial point of view, pumps typically rent for much less than a month's worth of formula.

He doesn't like me anymore, does he? Don't take the crying personally. If your baby fusses and cries during this process, keep in mind that learning is tough sometimes. He's not crying because you've done something wrong or because he doesn't like you. Quite the opposite. He adores you. He just doesn't like change. (Welcome to the human race, little man.) He'll love it when he learns it. One day he will probably fuss and cry about Algebra, and you'll respond to that with a kiss on the head, extra time helping him with homework, and maybe a session with a tutor. And so it goes with transitioning back to the breast. For some, it's a breeze. For those needing a little extra instruction and education, they'll do just fine with a patient mommy and maybe a session with a breastfeeding "tutor". Stay calm and confident. Think back to the days when you were tempted to quit breastfeeding. You didn't! You are a breastfeeding mom!

References

1. Meier P, et al. Nipple Shields for Preterm Infants: Effect on Milk Transfer and Duration of Breastfeeding. *Journal of Human Lactation* 2000;16(2):106-114.
2. Genna C, Nyqvist K. *Supporting Sucking Skills*, 2013; 187.
3. Mohrbacher N, Kendall-Tackett K. *Breastfeeding Made Simple.* 2010: 13-18.
4. Karon, A. Prompt frenotomy helps nursing for mom, baby. *Pediatric News* 2014; 12.
5. Knox, I. Tongue Tie and Frenotomy in the Breastfeeding Newborn. *NeoReviews* 2011;11;e513.
6. Buryk, M, Bloom D, Shope, T. Efficacy of Neonatel Release of Ankyloglossia: A Randomized Trial. *Pediatrics* 2011;128;280.
7. Berry J, Griffiths M, Westcott C. A double-blind, randomized controlled trial of tongue-tie division and its immediate effect on breastfeeding. *Breastfeeding Medicine* 2012;7(3):189-193.
8. Dollberg S, Marom R, Botzer E. Lingual frenotomy for breastfeeding difficulties: a prospective follow-up study. *Breastfeeding Medicine* 2014;9(6):286-289.
9. Geddes D, Langton D, Gollow I, et al. Frenotomy for breastfeeding infants with anykyloglossia: effect on milk removal and sucking mechanism as imaged by ultrasound. Pediatrics 2008b;2(1):e188-194.
10. Geddes D, Kent J, Mitoulas L, et al. Tongue movement and intra-oral vacuum in breastfeeding infants. *Early Human* Development 2008a;84(7):471-477.
11. Geddes D, Kent J, McClellan H, et al. Sucking characteristics of successfully breastfeeding infants with ankyloglossia: a case series. *Acta Paediatrica* 2010;99(2):301-303.
12. Hogan M, Westcott C, Griffiths M. Randomized, controlled trial of division of tongue tie in infants with feeding problems. *Journal of Paediatric and Child Health* 2005;41(5-6):246-250.
13. O'Callahan C, et al. 2013 The effects of office based frenotomy for anterior and posterior ankyloglossia on breastfeeding. *Journal of Pediatric Otorhinolaryngology* 77; 827-832.

Plugged Milk Ducts and Mastitis

Contact your lactation consultant and obstetrician *if you are experiencing breast pain and any of the following:*

- *you are less than 2 weeks postpartum*
- *nipple trauma is present*
- *you see blood or pus in milk*
- *one or both breasts has a reddened area*
- *your temperature increases suddenly*
- *you feel like you're coming down with the flu*

Bedrest is key for prevention and treatment of inflammation in the breasts, plugged milk ducts, and breast infection (mastitis). If you are resting in bed, the swelling in your body resolves more quickly and your body's energy can be used for fighting infection and healing. Ask for and accept help at home for a few days.

Reduce swelling around the affected area with bed rest and an anti-inflammatory medication. Ibuprofen (brand names are Motrin or Advil) is preferred while breastfeeding.[1] Ask your obstetrician about dosage and use. Cold compresses are also key to reducing swelling. Green cabbage leaves, if you are not allergic to cabbage, can be placed on top of the affected area of the breast inside your bra. Replace the leaves when they wilt. Apply the leaves continuously until the breasts are comfortable. Cabbage does not reduce milk supply. Leaving milk in the breasts reduces milk supply.

Moist heat and gentle massage before nursing or pumping can be helpful. A diaper filled with hot water is a quick, easy way to apply moist heat. Hold the diaper around the affected breast for several minutes before you nurse or pump. Gently massage breast from the base of the breast toward the nipple, paying special attention to the affected area.[2] Massage before and during nursing and pumping. Some mothers have found it helpful to gently use a vibrating toothbrush over the area to help "break up" the plug, aiding release of the milk.

Aggressively remove milk from your breasts until symptoms are relieved. This means frequent nursing or pumping - every 1-2 hours during the day and every 2-3 hours at night until feeling better.[2] If nursing, start on the affected breast. Pumping after nursing to aid breast drainage is also helpful.[3]

If it hurts to pump or if milk is not releasing well, check to see if your breast shield (flange) is fitted properly. If it is too small or too large, you may experience pain, and the milk may not release well. The size that is right for you may change over time. For help finding your best fit, refer to **Proper Breast Flange Fit** page 88.

When pumping, pump one side at a time, gently massaging from the affected area toward the nipple with your free hand. Coconut or olive oil may be used on the breast to aid massage. They may also be applied to the nipples prior to pumping to aid comfort. You can lean forward while nursing or pumping, using gravity to help move the plug. If you see something on the tip of your nipple that looks like a "milk blister", contact your IBCLC or obstetrician for further instructions. It is common to see thick or stringy milk when a plug is being released from the breast. It is ok to continue nursing your baby.

Probiotics can help your immune system fight infection. Lactobacillus GG is a type of good bacteria that has been well studied and widely recommended by healthcare providers. Ask your obstetrician how much probiotic you should take.

Lecithin capsules can aid milk release. Lecithin is not a medicine; it is a nutritional supplement. Recommended dosage is one to two 1200 mg capsule 3-4 times daily until your symptoms resolve, then taper gradually.[2,4] If you produce a large volume of milk, you may want to continue once daily if you develop a recurrence of the symptoms.[5] Your IBCLC can provide more information as needed. Check with your healthcare provider if you have medical problems.

Anticipate a minor and brief **reduction in milk volume** until your symptoms are resolved. Your baby may need to nurse a little more often during this time. Contact your lactation consultant and physician if a decreased supply persists more than a week.

Continue to **protect your rest** after symptoms resolve to avoid recurrence. If your symptoms do recur, consult your lactation consultant to review possible causes.

References

1. Reece-Stremtan S, Campos M, Kokajko L, and the Academy of Breastfeeding Medicine. *Breastfeeding Medicine*. November 2017,12(9):500-506.
2. Mohrbacher, N. *Breastfeeding Answers Made Simple* 2010: 659, 682-686.
3. Amir L, and the Academy of Breastfeeding Medicine Protocol Committee. *Breastfeeding Medicine*. June 2014,9(5):239-243.
4. Newman J, Pitman T. *The Ultimate Breastfeeding Book of Answers* 2006. Three Rivers Press.
5. www.kellymom.com. Accessed February 2018.

Safe Weaning

Whether you are weaning from breast feeding or pumping, allowing your body to gradually decrease milk production is a healthy approach for mom and baby. If you need emotional or physical support during this process or if you change your mind about weaning, call your IBCLC.
Remember to always refer to yourself as having been a breastfeeding mom.
Any breastmilk of a breastfeeding mom provided to your baby earns you the title.
Well done!

- Start by pumping or nursing a few minutes less than you typically would. Decrease the number of minutes as your body allows. Wear a supportive bra day and night until your breasts are comfortable, but avoid binding your breasts. Cool compresses will help decrease discomfort. Unless you are allergic, green cabbage leaves are especially helpful. Place leaves inside your bra. Change the leaves every 1-2 hours. Also ask your healthcare provider about taking Ibuprofen to relieve pain and inflammation.

- Offer your baby supplemental milk (previously expressed breast milk or formula) during the process of weaning from the breast.

- Gradually lengthen the time between nursing and/or pumping sessions at the rate your body will allow. You may find that you will be able to go longer in the late afternoon and evening.

- When you get down to one morning session and one evening session, drop the evening one first and then the morning one.

- If you need to wean more quickly, sage extract and pseudoephedrine (Sudafed) have been reported to decrease milk volume.[1] One study showed that even a single dose of pseudoephedrine (Sudafed) has been shown to significantly decrease overall milk volume.[2] The recommended starting dose is 30 mg and, if you do not experience irritability or sleeping problems, you can increase to 60 mg twice daily (once every 12 hours) for three days.[3] **Check with your physician before taking this medication, if you have high blood pressure or heart rate problems.**

- Oral contraceptives (birth control pills) containing estrogen and other hormonal forms of birth control (some IUD's, patch) can suppress your breast milk production hormone and help you wean more quickly if needed.[1] Talk with your physician.

- Since leaving some milk in the breast is the way your body gets the message to produce less milk, you are at increased risk for plugged milk ducts. Monitor your breasts for plugged milk ducts. Call your physician if you develop intense pain in one or both breasts, fever, chills, or aching. These can be symptoms of mastitis. See **Plugged Ducts and Mastitis** page 56.

- Consult with your pediatrician regarding introducing infant formula. Family history of food allergy is important to take into consideration when making the choice. It may ease the transition for your baby to blend the formula and expressed breastmilk together during the weaning process.

- If your baby is excessively fussy after transitioning to full formula feeds, make an appointment with your pediatrician for examination and further advice.

- If you are weaning an older infant who has come to depend upon nursing to fall asleep or fall back to sleep, seek advice from your pediatrician, IBCLC, and/or mother's support group.

- Call your obstetrician, pediatrician, and/or IBCLC with any questions or concerns.

References

1. Bevens P, Eglash A, Malloy M, Steube A, and the Academy of Breastfeeding Medicine. *Breastfeeding Medicine.* March 2016, 11(2):46-53.
2. Aljaza, I, Hale T, Ilett K, Hartmann P, Mitoulas L, Kristensen J, Hackett L. Pseudoephedrine: effects on milk production in women and estimation of infant exposure via breastmilk. *Br J Clin Pharmacol*. 2003 Jul;56(1):18-24.
3. Eglash A. Treatment of maternal hypergalactia. *Breastfeeding Medicine* 2014; 9(9):423-425.

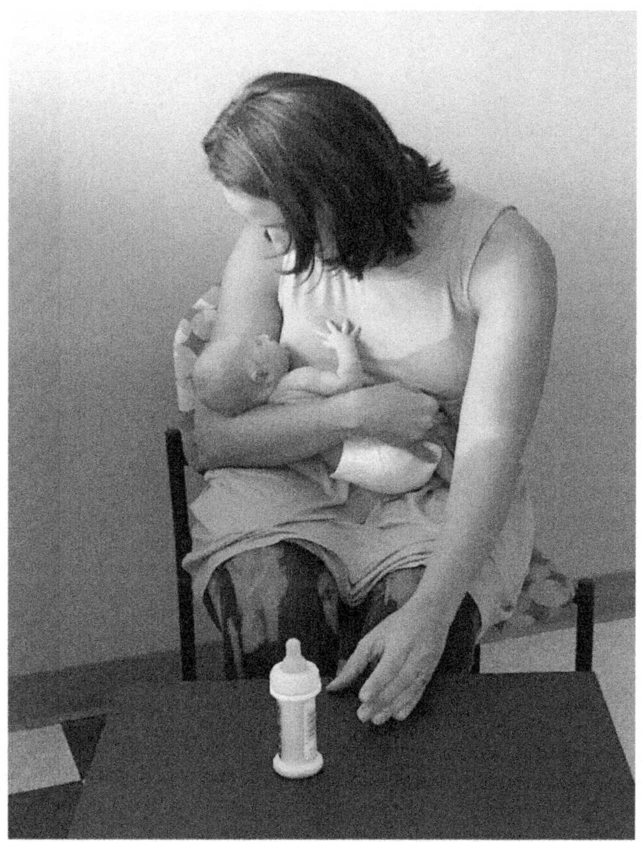

Part 3

Making Sense of it All

The Challenges

It's ok if you need extra help and your baby needs extra milk

Why doesn't breastfeeding seem to work as well for me as it does for other moms? Why does every doctor, nurse, and lactation consultant tell me something different? These two questions are frequently and validly asked. Why indeed? Because you are an individual and your baby is an individual, but you may feel like you are being forced into a box without options. Perhaps you and your baby's risk factors have not been fully taken into consideration (see pages 64,65). Or maybe no one has asked you what *your* goals are. Be honest about your intention to breastfeed and/or formula feed so that your healthcare providers can counsel you accordingly. No one set of instructions applies to breastfeeding, just as no one set of instructions applies to labor and delivery. The ideal birth is at 40 weeks vaginally, but of course we don't expect all babies to be born vaginally at 40 weeks because it involves too many variables that are beyond our control. Breastfeeding involves even more variables that are beyond our control, so the same flexible expectations should apply.

Breastfeeding is natural, but it doesn't come naturally. Research tells us that breast-feeding challenges are very common, even for moms completely committed to breastfeeding.[1,2] Expect a few glitches early on and engage your sense of humor.

The instructions you receive may have been appropriate for another mother in another situation in another room down the hall, but if those instructions don't feel right to you, **it's ok to ask for another option**. Don't allow yourself to become so overwhelmed that you end up wanting to quit. When you're having your second baby, you'll naturally be more confident, but with your first you are understandably less confident.[3] Myths, lack of information, and conflicting information can cause confusion and frustration. Understanding what some of the common challenges to breastfeeding success are and how to tackle them will empower you to think logically and follow your instincts. Being armed with correct and individualized information helps decrease your stress level so you can better enjoy your first baby.

Don't panic if things aren't going the way you pictured. You may be told that your baby needs some extra milk in the form of expressed breast milk and/or infant formula. The lists on pages 64 and 65 will help explain why your baby may need a flexible feeding plan, maybe even some supplemental nutrition for the short or long term. The lists have been compiled from Rebecca Mannel's acuity level classification from Oklahoma University Medical Center[4] and expanded with risk factors identified in protocols from the Academy of Breastfeeding Medicine. [5-7]

Breastfeeding challenges are categorized as **low risk**, **moderate risk**, or **high risk**. Moderate and high risk situations require expert breastfeeding support from an IBCLC. For example, high risk breastfeeding families can anticipate the likelihood of their baby needing some extra milk, which would likely include the need for a multiple-user rental breast pump and individualized plans of care. There is also a listing of risk factors categorized according to the challenges they may provide. When prepared for the possible challenge, you can be armed with the appropriate plan of care.

These "risk factors" do not mean that you are not going to be able to breastfeed. They just mean that you will benefit from expert lactation support while you're in the hospital and until any breastfeeding or milk supply challenges have been conquered. Each situation has a general plan of care. Your individual situation will have an individual plan of care based upon your progress.

Low Risk Breastfeeding Situations

- Mother with healthy, full term baby and previous breastfeeding experience
- Vaginal birth without intervention (minimal IV fluid, no labor medication)
- Mother and infant not separated
- Maternal pain controlled by non-opioid medication such as Ibuprofen
- Baby latches to the breast with minimal assistance and feels confident about progress
- Mother desires to pump and feed expressed breast milk and/or formula
- Minimal interruption of rest and feedings by visitors and hospital activities

Moderate Risk Breastfeeding Situations

- First-time breastfeeding mother with healthy, full-term baby
- Caesarian section delivery
- Vaginal birth interventions (such as having an epidural, multiple bags IV fluid, multiple doses IV antibiotics, forceps or vacuum delivery, prolonged pushing stage of labor)
- Delayed first feeding (defined as after 1 hour with vaginal delivery and 2 hours with routine Caesarean section)
- Non-first-time mother who previously experienced breastfeeding difficulty
- Maternal age (less than 18 or more than 35)
- Maternal chronic conditions (such as obesity, hypertension, cancer, rheumatoid arthritis, lupus)
- Maternal endocrine disorders (such as infertility, gestational or pre-pregnancy diabetes, thyroid disorders, polycystic ovarian syndrome - PCOS)
- Maternal acute illness/conditions (such as postpartum swelling and edema in extremities including breasts, preeclampsia, postpartum hemorrhage, postpartum depression, active infection)

- Maternal medications. Ask your prescriber to look up the medication on LactMed, a free online resource and smart phone app provided by the NIH. For the most detailed information, refer to *Medications and Mother's Milk* by Thomas Hale, PhD.
- Maternal physical or mental disability
- Infant latching difficulties (as evidenced by maternal nipple pain or poor breastfeeding assessment scores)
- Infant birth trauma (bruising or difficult delivery)
- Inadequate milk transfer from mother leading to medical recommendation to supplement
- Separation of the infant from the mother for more than an hour for any reason
- Excessive visitors and hospital activities resulting in limited opportunity for maternal and infant quiet rest

High Risk Breastfeeding Situations

- High maternal anxiety
- Maternal breast conditions (i.e., history of breast surgery, breast/nipple abnormalities, no breasts changes during pregnancy)
- Maternal illness/surgery
- Severe breast engorgement or infection
- High-risk infant (**less than 38 weeks gestation**, multiples, baby is small or large for gestational age)
- Excessive infant jaundice
- Low infant blood sugars
- Congenital anomalies
- Infant illness or surgery
- Infant oral or motor problems (tongue tie, lip tie, low or high muscle tone)
- Infant admission to the Neonatal Intensive Care Unit (NICU)
- Infant weight loss greater than 7% of birth weight before discharge from hospital
- Separation of the infant from the mother for extended periods of time
- Excessive visitors and hospital activities resulting in limited opportunity for maternal and infant quiet rest

Risk factors for your milk coming in later than normal

Defined as your higher volume of milk "coming in" after 72 hours postpartum[1]
Studies show that 22% to 44% of women experience this[8,9]

- First time mom[1,10]
- Stressful, prolonged, or difficult delivery[1,11]
- Preterm delivery - prior to 38 weeks gestation[12,13]
- Cesarean birth[1]
- Retained placental fragments[1]
- Maternal medical conditions - such as obesity BMI > 29,[8,14] edema/swelling,[8,10,15] diabetes,[16] high blood pressure[10]
- Not having changes in your breasts during pregnancy (never felt sore or slightly larger)[16]
- Feeding baby non-breast milk fluids (water, infant formula) instead of nursing or feeding mom's pumped breast milk 8 or more times every 24 hours[1]
- Delayed or infrequent breast drainage[17]
- "Sleepy baby" (shut-down baby) who is not nursing actively and effectively[15]

Risk factors for breasts that are painful and not releasing milk well (Engorgement)

- **Prolonged labor** (particularly with epidural anesthesia) can result in longer exposure to IV fluids, increasing swelling in your body.[1,11]
- **Augmented labor** (Pitocin in your IV during labor) may increase swelling in your body.[18]
- **Breast surgery** – both augmentation and reduction can affect breast drainage.[19,20]
- **Swelling in your extremeties** (including your breasts) can be a normal result of naturally higher sodium levels during pregnancy and increased fluid circulation in early postpartum. Additional swelling can occur if you had IV fluids during your labor.[21] If your swelling is severe or you have a history of high blood pressure, contact your obstetrician. Note: postpartum blood pressure is highest three to six days after birth.[22]
- **Overactivity** - If you are up and moving a lot during your first days postpartum, your body will have more difficulty eliminating swelling in your extremities (your breasts are extremities just like your ankles). Bed rest is the best advice for a mother experiencing swelling anywhere in her body. Gravity can be your enemy or your friend.
- **The "sleepy" baby** who is not nursing actively may not be effectively draining the breasts.[15]
- **Limited breast drainage** due to persistent latching difficulty, lack of practice with hand expression, or ineffective breast pump[17]

Risk factors for baby struggling to get sufficient milk (the #1 reason moms wean before they want to)

- Prematurity - Defined as less than 37 weeks gestation. This is a contributing factor to increasing the likelihood of sub-optimal feedings due to "sleepiness" and/or jaundice. You might consider these babies as wishing they were still receiving passive nutrition from the placenta.[12]
- Jaundice or Hypoglycemia (low blood sugar) - until resolved, baby is not typically an alert and vigorous feeder.[23]
- Ineffective latch or suck - baby is typically alert and willing but unable to nurse effectively.[2]
- Tongue tie or other anatomical challenges such as a poor fit of mom's nipple in baby's mouth - again, baby may be alert and willing, but unable.[24]
- Long intervals between feedings - if mother is intentionally limiting access to the breast or if baby is "too sleepy" to wake for at least 8 feedings every 24 hours in the first week.
- Baby receives bottles of formula **without mother receiving adequate breast stimulation and drainage for establishment of milk supply**.[1]
- "Sleepy baby" (shut-down baby) who is not nursing actively or effectively[15]

Risk factors for nipple/breast pain or infection (the #2 reason moms wean before they want to)

- Nipple skin damage- This can be due to poor latch to breast, poor pumping technique, or ineffective pump motor.[25]
- Unrelieved breast engorgement- This can be due to poor latch to breast, limitation of nursing/pumping, or severe edema creating a "sucking milk through a pinched straw" situation which contributes to milk being left in the breast.[25]
- Exposure to antibiotics before, during, or after labor can decrease your amount of "good" bacteria along with the bad, which can allow other organisms like yeast to overgrow. Studies have shown that 30% to 60% of moms are treated with IV antibiotics, which increases mom and baby's risk of yeast/thrush infection.[26]

You sense there is a problem

Even if you are not experiencing any of the above problems, but still sense that your baby is not nursing well enough to bring your milk in or get your milk out, **trust your own assessment**. Refer back to the **Breastfeeding Challenge Flowchart** on pages 8,9 for help specific to your situation. **When in doubt, pump.**

References

1. Dewey KG, Nomssen-Rivers LA, Heinig MJ, Cohen RJ. Risk factors for suboptimal infant feeding behavior, delayed onset of lactation, excess neonatal weight loss. *Pediatrics* 2003 Sep; 12(3 Pt 1):607-19.
2. Stuebe AM, Horton BJ, Chetwynd E, Watkins S, Grewen K, Meltzer-Brody S. Prevalence and risk factors for early, undesired weaning attributed to lactation dysfunction. *J Womens Health* 2014 May;23(5):404-12.
3. Gerhardsson E, Nyqvist K, Mattsson E, Volgsten H, Hildingsson I, Funkquist EL. Breastfeeding Self-Efficacy Scale Assessment. *Journal of Human Lactation* 2014 Aug;30(3):340-345.
4. Mannel, R. Defining Lactation Acuity to Improve Patient Safety and Outcomes. *Journal of Human Lactation* 2011;27(2):163-170.
5. Evans A, Marinelli K, Taylor JS, and the Academy of Breastfeeding Medicine. *Breastfeeding Medicine*. January 2014;9(1):3-8.
6. Kellams A, Harrel C, Omage S, Gregory C, Rosen-Carole C, and the Academy of Breastfeeding Medicine. *Breastfeeding Medicine*. May 2017;12(4):188-198.
7. Reece-Stremtan S, Campos M, Kokajko L, and the Academy of Breastfeeding Medicine. *Breastfeeding Medicine*. November 2017;12(9):500-506.
8. Nommsen-Rivers LA, Chantry CJ, Peerson JM, et al. Delayed onset of lactogenesis among first time mothers is related to maternal obesity and factors associated with ineffective breastfeeding. *American Journal of Clinical Nutrition* 2010;92(3):574-584.
9. Chapman DJ, Perez-Escamilla R. Identification of risk factors for delayed onset of lactation. *Journal of the American Dietetic Association* 1999;99(4):450-454.
10. Hall R, Mercer A, Teasley S, et al. A breastfeeding assessment score to evaluate the risk for cessation of breastfeeding by 7-10 days of age. *Journal of Pediatrics* 2002;141(5):659-664.
11. Chen D, Nommsen-Rivers LA, Dewey KG, Lonnerdal B. Stress during labor and delivery and early lactation performance. *The American Journal of Clinical Nutrition* 1998;68(2):335-344.
12. Parker LA, Sullivan S, Krueger C, Kelechi T, Mueller M. Effect of early breast milk expression on milk volume and timing of lactogenesis stage II among mothers of very low birth weight infants: a pilot study. *Journal of* Perinatology 2012;32(2):205-209.
13. Parker LA, Sullivan S, Krueger C, et al. Association of timing of initiation of breastmilk expression on milk volume and timing of lactogenesis stage II among mothers of very low birth weight infants. *Breastfeeding Medicine* 2015;10(2):84-91.
14. Rasmussen K, Kjolhede C. Prepregnant overweight and obesity diminish the prolactin response to sucking in the first week postpartum. *Pediatrics* 2004;113(5):e465-470.
15. Wilson-Clay B, Hoover K. *The Breastfeeding Atlas* 2017: 8-9,76.
16. Riddle SW, Nommsen-Rivers LA. A case control study of diabetes during pregnancy and low milk supply. *Breastfeeding Medicine* 2016;11(2):1-6.
17. Becker GE, Smith HA, Cooney F. Methods of milk expression for lactating women. *Cochrane Database System Review* 2016;2:CD006170. DOI:10.1002/14651858.
18. http://dailymed.nlm.nih.gov/dailymed/druginfo.cfm. (PITOCIN-oxytocin injection). Accessed February 2018.
19. Hurst N. Lactation after augmentation mammoplasty. *Obstetrics and Gynecology* 1996;87(1):30-34.
20. Cruz NI, Korchin L. Lactational performance after breast reduction with different pedicles. *Plastic Reconstructive Surgery* 2007;(20)1:35-40.
21. Ghuman N, Rheiner J, Tendler B, White W. Hypertension in the Postpartum Woman: Clinical Update for the Hypertension Specialist. *The Journal of Clinical Hypertension* 2009; 11(12):726-733.
22. Magee L, Sadeghi S, von Dadelszen P. Prevention and treatment of postpartum hypertension. *Cochrane Database of Systemic Reviews* 2005, Issue 1. Art No.:CD004351.
23. Wight N, Marinelli K, and the Academy of Breastfeeding Medicine. *Breastfeeding Medicine* May 2014; 9(4):173-179.
24. The Academy of Breastfeeding Medicine Protocol Committee. Guidelines for the evaluation and management of neonatal ankyloglossia and its complications in the breastfeeding dyad. August 2004. www.bfmed.org. Accessed Feb 2018.
25. Amir L, and the Academy of Breastfeeding Medicine Protocol Committee. *Breastfeeding Medicine*. June 2014, 9(5):239-243.
26. Sasaki, B (2014). Does Lanolin Use Increase the Risk for Infection in Breastfeeding Women? *Clinical Lactation 5(1);* 28-32.

The Priorities

The only thing we can't fix later is your milk supply

In the fog of childbirth followed by conflicting advice, it's easy to lose sight of the goal or the "main thing". The "main thing" for any parent learning how to feed a newborn is to ***enjoy your baby***. The next big thing for a breastfeeding family is to arrive on the other side of breastfeeding challenges with **all your options still open**. A fog-clearing approach used by breastfeeding experts Barbara Wilson-Clay and Kay Hoover reflects three priorities to consider while working through your challenges:

1. Feed the baby.
2. Protect the milk supply.
3. Protect the breastfeeding relationship.[1,2]

Start thinking in terms of **long term success**. Exclusively feeding your baby from the breast is ideal in the first few weeks. If breastfeeding exclusively from the breast is working well for you, that's fantastic. But if you are struggling and feel required or even strongly encouraged to prioritize exclusively feeding at the breast without consideration of your individual situation, you may experience heightened anxiety and needless frustration. "Just keep nursing" is likely to be an inadequate plan of care when you are facing breastfeeding challenges, particularly in regard to protecting milk supply.[3] **Ironically, if you or your baby is struggling, prioritizing your direct breastfeeding relationship over protecting your milk supply *may actually risk* your long-term milk supply AND breastfeeding relationship.**[4-12]

However, if you are given options and empowered to conquer challenges, you are more likely to achieve your goals. See **Challenges Flowchart** on pages 8,9. **Reject the fear that you are "doing it wrong"**. The priority approach keeps all your options open for long term success no matter what happens in the short term.[13] **You just need a do-able plan.**

Priority # 1 = Feed the baby

The truly low risk breastfeeding family is a family who conceives without intervention, gives birth without intervention, and breastfeeds without intervention. This is a rarity today. Our healthcare system recognizes that high risk pregnancy requires a different plan of care. Physicians have developed a medical specialty for high risk pregnancy, and hospitals have made policies that reflect this reality. The reality continues when the high risk pregnant mother becomes a high risk mother. That's where the disconnect seems to happen. We need risk assessment to continue as pregnancy and birth become breastfeeding and bonding to avoid an all-or-nothing breastfeeding message for mothers who very much want to breastfeed. Well-meaning global and national breastfeeding exclusivity policies for hospitals and community clinics[16] do not yet reflect the on-going need for individualized plans of care for mothers at risk for unintended weaning. [14,15,16]

Often, therefore, healthcare policy does not match human reality. Some things are simply beyond our control. Just like you can't expect every baby to be born at 40 weeks vaginally, neither can you expect every baby in the normal newborn nursery to exclusively breastfeed. You can't force every baby to nurse often and effectively. Neither can you force every mother's body to produce milk quickly enough to maintain exclusive breastfeeding at the time of discharge from the hospital and beyond. And, in terms of global policy, what may be helpful for a mother in a developing country may not apply to mothers who have access to many resources.

What this means for you as a new parent is that you should **trust your instincts**. Advocate for yourself and your baby until there is a policy change that assesses for risk and adjusts care accordingly.

If you sense that your baby isn't nursing well or would just like to have a little more milk, you can hand express colostrum and feed it to your baby in a spoon. Ask the nurses and IBCLCs at the hospital to help you. Practicing hand expression helps you learn your breasts and become a little more comfortable with the process of breastfeeding. You can watch a video of hand expression and hands-on pumping at https://med.standford.edu/newborns/professional-education/breastfeeding/maximizing-milk-production.html . Doing both hand expression and pumping is more effective than pumping by itself.[17]

If you are past 48 hours and are experiencing any of the warning signs listed below, the baby may not be getting enough milk yet.[18] Consult with your pediatrician and IBCLC as soon as possible. Use the **Milk Journals** on page 97 and refer to the **Challenges Flowchart** on pages 8 and 9 for specific guidance.

Warning signs for a baby older than 48 hours

- There are consistently fewer than 8 or more than 16 feedings per 24 hours.
- Feedings are consistently shorter than 5 minutes or longer than 30 minutes.[19]
- There is rapid sucking with little to no swallowing most of the time.
- Baby sucks 3-4 times, falls asleep, stays at the breast, and repeats this pattern.
- Mother's nipple is creased, cracked, flattened, blanched, or painful after feeding.
- Breast fullness doesn't change (soften) as a result of the feeding.
- Baby isn't pooping (larger than quarter size) 3 or more times per 24 hours.
- Baby's weight loss is greater than 7% of birth weight.[12]

While you are working through your breastfeeding challenges, feeding your baby is priority # 1. It's ok if your baby needs extra milk and a mommy needs extra stimulation before breastfeeding is fully established. Typically, the **extra milk is needed in small volumes for a short time**. You may have concerns about brief or extended periods of bottle feeding extra milk (either your pumped breast milk or infant formula). Several of those concerns are addressed next.

What about nipple confusion?

Nipple "confusion" is commonly defined as a refusal of the breast following introduction of an artificial nipple. *"Nipple preference"* might be a better term for this problem since "confusion" is not an ideal definition of behavior that indicates a nipple preference. Nor is it an ideal definition of feeding behavior that indicates a baby is actually *unable* to breastfeed in the short or long term[20]. Mothers' fear of short or long term breast refusal may be lessened by knowing that there is a study showing that some babies can go back and forth easily.[21] But if your baby struggles, stay positive and know that "with information, reassurance, and effective case management, most problems can be corrected over time, and the baby can receive mother's milk until direct breastfeeding is established".[22]

Also, there is one major aspect of bottle nipple preference that has not been studied-- nipple protractility, meaning the ability of mom's nipple to stretch into the back of the baby's mouth. The sensation of mom's nipple in the back of the mouth is what elicits the strong reflex for suckling. Things that can interfere with nipple protractility are flat or inverted nipples and breast engorgement. Bottle nipples automatically stimulate the back of the baby's mouth, eliciting the strong sucking reflex. For the baby whose mother has poor nipple protractility, the breasts "can't compete".[23] Sometimes a nipple shield is helpful for this challenge. See **Nipple Shield Use** page 34.

If your baby is not able to easily transition back and forth between breast and bottle, keep in mind that nipple preference occurring in the first few weeks is a problem that can be overcome in time. Failing to fully establish milk supply in the first few weeks can be very difficult or even impossible to overcome.

Remember the 3 priorities. In order for a breastfeeding relationship to be established and thrive, milk must be removed from mother's breasts and taken in by the baby. Research shows that establishing an adequate supply for the long term requires *frequent and complete breast drainage in the first 3 weeks, with **the most critical time being the first few days.***[24,25] So, if you use a nipple shield, pump after nursing to ensure complete breast drainage. See **Nipple Shield Use** on page 34. If direct breastfeeding isn't going well yet, choosing the appropriate breast pump for your situation is very important. See **Right Pump for You** on page 40.

The reality is that in the short term (rarely in the long term), there are situations in which frequent and complete breast drainage cannot happen via direct breastfeeding alone. If that is the case, the use of an *artificial nipple* for the *short term* is better than the use of *artificial breast milk* (infant formula) for the *long term*.

What about alternative feeding methods?

When small volumes of extra milk (pumped breast milk or infant formula) are needed for a limited amount of time, an alternative feeding method such as a syringe or cup may be appropriate. An example of a useful time to try an alternative feeding method is if you're just trying to get through a period of 12-24 hours until mom's milk comes in. However, you must be trained how to safely feed the extra milk by a knowledgeable breastfeeding helper. In cases where larger volumes of extra milk are needed or when the extra milk is needed for longer than 24 hours, a more familiar feeding method (bottles) may be more helpful. Alternative feeding methods should be individualized. [12,26,27]

"An optimal supplemental feeding device has not yet been identified, and may vary from one infant to another. No method is without potential risk or benefit. When selecting an alternative feeding method, clinicians should consider several criteria: cost and availability, ease of use and cleaning, stress to the infant, whether adequate milk volume can be fed in 20-30 minutes, whether anticipated use is short- or long-term, maternal preference, and whether the method enhances development of breast-feeding skills".[12]

If your baby is thriving and you are comfortable using alternate feeding methods approved by your pediatrician and taught to you by a knowledgeable breastfeeding helper, by all means continue. But if you aren't comfortable or you're overwhelmed, **the bottle is not your enemy**. Don't be afraid to use a bottle but do take the time to learn how to use a bottle safely and effectively. Bottles may be your bridge to success.[28]

Bottles can save breastfeeding!

As long as you continue draining your breasts with an appropriate breast pump (see **Right Pump for You** page 40 and **Pumping Tips** page 89), you are protecting your breast milk supply (see **Priority #2** page 76). The key is to seek assistance from an IBCLC when it is time to transition the baby back to directly feeding from the breast as described in **Going Back to the Breast** page 51. Babies can learn to breastfeed as long as there is plenty of milk in the breast.[26]

What about the importance of breastfeeding exclusivity?

Breastfeeding your baby in his first week of life without the use of bottles, pacifiers, and infant formula may be optimal, but it is **not a realistic expectation for all** mothers and babies. In the current optimal infant feeding culture, if exclusive breastfeeding is not achievable for you in the short or long term, you've heard a message of failure rather than the message of success. Sadly, that could discourage you from persisting with *any* breastfeeding, rather than giving you options that would support continued breastfeeding for as much as and as long as possible.[29]

An unintended consequence of current global and national breastfeeding policies[14-16] is that some mothers believe that they must choose between exclusive breastfeeding and zero breastfeeding. Non-individualized or conflicting advice from medical professionals, pressure from family members, comparison with social media contacts, a general fear that she is "doing it wrong", and a growing sadness that things aren't going the way she pictured can discourage a mother to the point that she bows her head in defeat. This state of mind and body could be considered maternal failure to thrive.

The understandable anxiety and distress she feels increases the circulation of stress hormones, which can make it difficult for a mother to connect with her newborn. However, maternal failure to thrive can be remedied. Hormones that are released as you relax and hold your baby can actually shift your brain from the side of details and data to the side of connection and calm.[30] When you start to discover how you and your baby were designed to function together, you will sense that things are starting to go right.

Researchers explain that "when the mother herself is in a calm and relaxed state, she is open to subtle communication with her newborn; she can connect and respond to her infant's behavior and with her response transfer that calm state regulation to her infant".[31] If mom thrives, baby thrives. Basically, your baby is waiting for you to go first. But how do you go first? You need the people around you to care for you, so that you can care for your baby.

If the people around you aren't automatically caring for you, or they are trying and you won't let them, ask for and accept their help. Then cut off the old negative messages, hold your baby, and trust your instincts. If the two of you settle into a breastfeeding relationship that feels right to you, that's fantastic. Keep moving forward together. If you sense that you and your baby need some different options, even if just for the short term, trust your instincts on that too. One study found that "maternal confidence was a stronger predictor of breastfeeding outcome than supplementation or perception of support".[32,33]

One logical option to protect your supply is to express your own breast milk with a quality breast pump and feed that milk to your baby in bottles until "the infant is competent to maintain production",[34] or as stated in this book, "the baby is ready for primetime". If needed, you can offer limited volumes of infant formula in addition to your milk in bottles until your milk supply is fully established. Consult your pediatrician for specific feeding amount recommendations for your baby, as these may change daily. Also see **Milk Journals** page 97 and **Bottles, Pacifiers, and Formula** page 45. Even for healthy, low risk moms and babies, problems (like nipple trauma, breast pain, or infant jaundice) may arise that *require having options in order to be successful.*

Regardless of whether or not it is ideal, **if** the pumping-into-bottles option is what is needed right now to calm both you and your baby, then it **is** the right option for you. Especially if you are in a moderate or high risk category (see pages 64, 65), pumping and bottle feeding provide a "life preserver" for a few days or even a few weeks (see **Combination Feeding Option** page 36). You don't have to stop breastfeeding, but you can pump instead of nursing for as many feedings as you need to for as long as you need to. Ensure that you have the appropriate breast pump for the number of feedings you need to replace daily (see **Right Pump for You** page 40 and **Milk Journals** page 97). This option **buys you some time** to work through your breastfeeding challenges without losing your milk supply. Instead of decreasing your confidence in your ability to provide milk for you baby, your confidence might actually be boosted as you see **your milk** calming your baby. This plan is not forever. With a full milk supply and a baby who is ready, you can go on to a satisfying, often exclusive, breastfeeding relationship with your current baby as well as future babies[35] (see **Going Back to the Breast** page 51). *The Breastfeeding Atlas* explains that "the transition to direct, exclusive breastfeeding is always easier if there is ample milk supply and if the babies are not calorie deprived".[36]

Nipple shields can be very useful tools if baby is refusing the breast or if baby is able to breastfeed, but mom is experiencing pain. However, until you are certain that your milk supply is well-established and the baby is consistently gaining well, nipple shield use requires regular follow up with your IBCLC's continued assessment of your baby's suck. Also, until your baby is able to nurse effectively, "insurance pumping" is needed after nursing.[37] This means draining breasts after nursing with a high-quality breast pump to protect your milk supply. Shields can also be helpful for preterm infants who tire easily at the breast.[38] But, again, insurance pumping is needed to protect supply. Follow up with your pediatrician and IBCLC to monitor your baby for appropriate weight gain. See **Nipple Shield Use** page 34.

If you feel strongly about not introducing artificial nipples or infant formula but are experiencing difficulty, meet in person with an IBCLC early and often. She will work with you to ensure proper breast stimulation for you and adequate nutrition for your baby. It is not unusual for the struggling mom to meet and/or speak with her lactation consultant daily during the first week postpartum. Never hesitate to reach out for help while the challenges are being conquered. And remember to trust your instincts.

For a number of reasons, not the least of which is reduced emotional stress, the goal of **exclusive** breastfeeding during the first week of life seems to be more naturally achieved by an **experienced** breastfeeding mother.[39] For a **first-time** mother, it may be helpful to think of it this way: the breastfeeding focus is building your *confidence* and achieving *your* breastfeeding *duration* goals. Then, when you are expecting your second baby, you can look forward to breastfeeding as an experienced mother. The breastfeeding focus for you can then be breastfeeding *exclusivity* in addition to *duration*. If you are a second (or third, etc.) time mother who had a traumatic experience the first time, just start at the beginning again with the focus on building confidence and achieving breastfeeding duration goals. Don't feel guilty or inferior if this is your second baby and you're not confident. You just need a few victories under your belt to build your confidence! You always have the option to wean on your own terms, but be comforted with the knowledge that bottles have saved breastfeeding for many families. Bottom line: What good is exclusivity without duration?

Will just a little formula hurt anything?

When you consider the importance of meeting your breastfeeding duration goals, perhaps the more important question is: Will a little formula **help** anything? If you're trying to protect your long-term breastfeeding **success** and you and your baby are experiencing multiple problems in the early days, a limited amount of formula may be a bridge to that success. Your pediatrician will advise you regarding any changes that need to be made to your feeding plan. One study suggests that early, limited volume (extensively hydrolyzed) formula does not jeopardize your short or long term breastfeeding goals and may actually help you to achieve your long-term goals.[35] Remember the importance of your connection with your baby and trust your instincts.

Just remember **formula = pumping**. In other words, if you are needing to use a little formula, you need to **also** be stimulating mom's body by hand expression and pumping. You probably will not express much milk at this stage of your lactation. The goal is to encourage your body to continue increasing production. Breast massage and the use of a quality breast pump are necessary to stimulate milk production.[40] Be patient and stay positive. Studies show that 22%-44% of mothers experience a delay in their milk coming in.[41,42] Many moms and babies need a safety net to help establish and protect milk supply while other challenges are being resolved. Expressing milk with your hands as well as with a high-quality breast pump **reduces your baby's exposure to formula** because you are draining your breasts better and growing **your milk** supply faster.[43] See **Combination Feeding Option** page 36 and **Right Pump for You** page 40.

The type of formula matters. According to the Academy of Breastfeeding Medicine, the ideal choice in the short term for all babies is an infant formula that is classified as hypo-allergenic.[40] These are dairy-based infant formulas, but the proteins are easier for your baby to digest and less likely to trigger an allergic response in your baby's gut. Choosing this type of formula is especially important for the baby with a family history of dairy protein allergy. An added benefit of the hypo-allergenic type of infant formula (research conducted with Enfamil's Nutramigen) is that it can be helpful in resolving infant jaundice. In other words, if your pediatrician advises a formula supplement during the first week of life, when jaundice is the most likely to occur (See **Jaundice** page 31), this type helps your baby to get rid of jaundice faster.[40,44-48] Also, they smell and taste even worse than the regular formulas, so your baby won't drink this formula for fun. The down-side is their cost, but if needed only for a short time, the expense is only for a short time. If you are unable to use this type of formula, ask your pediatrician for a recommendation.

The **amount** of extra milk (expressed breast milk or infant formula) needed varies with your breastfeeding situation. Common situations include:

- Your baby's day of life
- The degree of weight loss and/or jaundice
- The likelihood that your breastfeeding challenges will resolve in the near future
- The amount of milk your baby can currently transfer from the breast
- The number of times per day you are pumping
- The amount of milk you are able to express each day

Your pediatrician will guide you on the appropriate amount for your situation. A rule of thumb is to monitor the output of baby's poop as in indicator of how the baby is doing on intake of milk. Days 1-3 of life should see the same number of poops (i.e., the baby should poop 2 times on the 2nd day of life). A baby who is 4 days of age or older should poop 4 or more times per 24 hours (approximately every other feeding - more often is normal as well). Weight gain is the most objective indicator of adequate intake, but you can gauge if you're on the right track at home between pediatrician visits by counting poops. See **Milk Journals** page 97.

Keep in mind that your *second* baby may not need a single drop of infant formula. Your milk will most likely come in a little sooner and be a little higher in volume with your next baby. This prevents or solves many of the problems the first week presents. Plus, you won't be as fearful that you're going to do something wrong as you were with your first baby. When your second child has a problem, you'll look at your first one and say, "He turned out fine. This one will too." Confidence comes with time and experience. **Be patient with yourself and pretend you're having your *second* baby *first*.**

See **Combination Feeding Option** page 36 and **Milk Journals** page 97. Consult with your pediatrician for more specific guidance on supplementation with extra milk.

Priority # 2 = Protect Your Milk Supply

If you are in the category of **Low Risk Breastfeeding Situations** (see page 64) and your baby is consistently nursing well, that is great and you are probably not a first-time mom. Nursing well can be thought of as:

- You are not experiencing pain when you nurse.
- The baby is relaxed after nursing.
- The baby is gaining weight (after the normal initial loss).
- The baby is pooping 4 or more times every 24 hours by day 4 of life.

If any of the above does not apply to you, it's ok to embrace the reality that, as a parent, everything is not going to go exactly as you pictured. All parents deal with this reality at some point, so you are in good company. If either your body and/or your baby is not "ready for primetime", it is possible to establish and maintain your milk supply with a breast pump for the purpose of **buying you some time**. You can protect your milk supply for the long term while you work with an IBCLC to identify and conquer your specific challenges in the short term.

The specifics of how to get your milk in and keep it in with a breast pump until you're able to transition the baby back to the breast are included in **Combination Feeding Option** page 36, **Right Pump for You** page 40, **Milk Journals** page 97, and **Going Back to the Breast** page 51.

Key concepts for protecting your milk supply:

- You have basically one shot at establishing your milk supply, and **timing is everything**. The **critical first days and up to 3 weeks of age** are referred to as the **calibration phase** for your milk supply.[4-6,49,66] Without frequent and consistent breast drainage, the breast does not receive the maximum production signal. As a result, full milk supply potential may not be reached for the current breastfeeding relationship, which lactation consultants refer to as **"acquired low milk supply".**[50] If your baby is not nursing well enough to drain (fully soften) your breasts at each feeding, massage breasts and pump after nursing. Using a high-quality rental breast pump early and often gives you the best chance of success.[9,24,34,52] See **Right Pump for You** page 40 and **Combination Feeding Option** page 36.

- When you are experiencing breastfeeding difficulties, the key to long term success is effective breast drainage. To do that well enough and often enough, a multiple-user, large electric (hospital grade) **rental breast pump** is the optimal vehicle for success.[3,49,54,55] Experts advise "maintaining or increasing milk production by pumping with a hospital grade metal piston-driven breast pump at least 8 times each day."[56] "Hospital grade pumps" (large electric pumps safe for multiple-users) retail in the thousands of dollars and rent in the $75-$125/month range. Early establishment of a milk supply that is **more than the baby needs** is important.[57]

- During your first 10 days, your goal is to pump 8-12 times each 24-hours.

- A target for a full milk supply is the range of 25-35 ounces per day. Multiple studies confirm that the average long-term milk production for a healthy woman is approximately 800 milliliters (28 ounces) – with a range of up to 1200 milliliters (42 ounces).[58-60]

- Target volumes during the calibration phase for 24-hour total pumped milk amounts are 500 cc **by day 5** of life and 750-1000 cc by days 7-10 of life.[3,5,25,49,61-64] See **Milk Journals** page 97. If you are concerned about your milk supply, contact an IBCLC as soon as possible.

- "Hands on" techniques - breast compression and massage before and during breastfeeding and pumping - have been shown to **increase milk volumes**, increase milk fat content, and decrease milk expression time.[25,53] When expressing milk with a pump, increase vacuum setting only to the maximum level at which you are still comfortable.[3,65] Also listening to music while pumping and warming your breasts before pumping has been shown to increase your milk volumes.[25] See **Pumping Tips** on page 89.

- Until a full milk supply is established, your frequency of pumping is key to giving your body the right message. During the first 10 days, **8-12 sessions per 24 hours** is necessary. Each woman has a different **milk storage** capacity (how much milk your breasts are capable of storing at one time), so the number of times you will need to pump to reach the 24-hour target volumes will be individual to you[64]. Until the calibration phase is complete, maintaining at least 8 pumping sessions per 24 hours is ideal for establishing your individual maximum production. **The number of times you pump daily is more important than how long you pump**. Your body needs to receive the same message from the pump that it would be receiving from the baby. Therefore, you cannot pump less often than the baby is taking feedings (during the calibration phase). The work you do during the calibration phase puts you "in control of your breastfeeding destiny" since "increasing production is more difficult later".[63]

- The **costs of not breastfeeding** (formula costs, added healthcare costs, etc) far outweigh the costs of a breastfeeding success plan that includes breast pump rental costs, particularly when many families may only need to rent the pump for one month to help establish a full supply during the calibration phase. Many of the challenges to establishing a full milk supply listed in **Challenges** section (page 63) are **temporary** if conquered within the first week or two. Something to consider: the baby will never know if he missed a couple of toys or outfits in the first month of life. Perhaps a month's pump rental would be a good **gift suggestion**.

Priority # 3 = Protect the breastfeeding relationship

One important aspect of protecting the breastfeeding relationship is protecting the milk supply, **Priority #2** (page 76) But there are also steps you can take that will protect **Priority #3** (page 78), your baby's ability to smoothly transition back to breast feeding as soon as he is able.

The orders and locations of events matter

When you need to add supplementing with extra milk to your feeding routine, avoid advice that sabotages breastfeeding and seek advice that encourages breastfeeding. Ways of supplementing that encourage breastfeeding are detailed in **Combination Feeding Option** page

36. It is also helpful to understand that some of the controversy about supplementation, especially with bottles, is due to many mothers being unaware of potential risks to their breastfeeding relationship.

Supplementation **sabotages** breastfeeding in these situations:

- When infant **formula *replaces*** breast drainage altogether for even one of the baby's feedings, breastfeeding can be sabotaged. For example, if you're going to give your baby a bottle of extra milk and you are not going to put the baby to the breast first, you need to "drain" the breast as part of that feeding session with a high-quality breast pump. Even if you just get a few drops of milk when you pump, continue pumping on schedule for stimulation until your milk starts to increase in volume. See **Right Pump for You** page 40, **Combination Feeding Option** page 36, and **Milk Journals** page 97.

- When the bottles (or pacifiers for that matter) are not "breastfeeding friendly" in regard to their shape, flow rate, or the way they are introduced, they can sabotage breastfeeding. *Orthodontic shaped nipples are particularly important to avoid.* In order to keep an orthodontic-shaped pacifier in his mouth, he must keep his jaw clenched and his tongue pressed up against the nipple. Bottle and pacifier nipples that encourage your baby's jaw to remain open and tongue extended are less problematic. More info can be found in **Bottles, Pacifiers, and Formula** on page 45.

- If **ALL** bottles of extra milk are fed to the baby by someone other than you, breast-feeding can be sabotaged. **Make sure you are still spending time skin-to-skin for feedings**. You can bottle feed AT the breast prior to pumping. This contact with your baby can increase the amount of milk you are able to pump as a result of the release of a hormone called oxytocin. It works inside the breast to help release the milk.

- If the feeding routine takes **more than 45 minutes total** from start to finish, breast-feeding can be sabotaged. If you spend 30 minutes trying to nurse, then 20 minutes feeding extra milk via a bottle or alternative feeding device, then 20 minutes pumping plus cleaning parts/bottles, you have dedicated 1.25 hours to that feeding and the next one may be less than 1.25 hours away. This rhythm, referred to as "triple feeding", overwhelms nearly everyone and frequently backfires when you, understandably, drop the pumping portion of the routine in favor of more rest. Until your milk supply is fully established and the baby is "ready for primetime", your time and energy as well as the baby's is better spent focusing on Priorities #1 and #2 by **limiting the nursing minutes and maximizing the pumping minutes**.

Keep in mind that "breastfeeding cannot improve if the infant is **hungry or weak**. Many infants who appear to have sucking problems suck normally once they recover lost weight."[13]

How much you want to exclusively breastfeed matters

The assumption that all mothers who want to provide breast milk to their babies want to provide it exclusively at the breast may not be true for you. Be honest with your physicians, nurses, and IBCLC about your goals and the degree you wish to be flexible with the breastfeeding process. If you would like to exclusively pump milk for your baby for the long term, that can be achieved for most moms with the use of a multiple-user rental breast pump. If you want to supplement with formula long-term, ask how you can protect your breast milk supply. Work with your IBCLC toward achieving and maintaining your goals and remember that **breast-milk-feeding moms ARE breastfeeding moms**.

Where you get your help matters

The process of transitioning back to nursing directly from the breast as soon as possible is detailed in **Going Back to the Breast**, page 51. The person who helps you in this process can be just as important as the individual steps in the plan itself. Your baby may smoothly and swiftly return to feedings directly from the breast as soon as you both become stable and able. But if he is battling you at the breast, get help from a knowledgeable breastfeeding helper, someone who can help him develop this skill and has the ability to objectively assess his progress. During the transition, he may need weight checks and feeding observations in addition to obtaining gram weights before and after you nurse him.

Remember that a good predictor of how quickly he will be able to make the transition is his breastfeeding behavior prior to the crisis. Did he nurse well right after he was born? Did he nurse well until your milk started to come in? Did he nurse well until he started to become jaundiced? If so, that's great because that's really who he is. He'll remember what to do. He just needs a little time and patience.

On the other hand, if he didn't nurse well at the first feeding or you were experiencing pain with every breastfeeding, causing the need to change the feeding plan, he may need more time, more patience, and more evaluation. Have an IBCLC examine all the structures of his mouth. He could have something preventing him from being able to achieve a comfortable and effective latch. You can control only 50% of the equation (see **Newborn Magic Latch** page 13). He controls the other 50%, so it does little good to battle him in an attempt to achieve a latch that is not currently achievable, especially if your milk supply suffers and he associates the breast with frustration as a result. **Remember, first things first**. **Feed him and protect your supply**. The latch will come in time. You're not "doing it wrong". Both of you are learning how to do it. Seek help and persist until the right diagnosis is made and the right treatment plan is started.

If you are repeatedly unsuccessful at transitioning back to breastfeeding, ask your pediatrician about a referral to a professional who specializes in infant feeding problems.

See **Using This Book** page 4 for info on how to locate an IBCLC.

Remember to keep the main thing the main thing.

Above all else, enjoy your baby!!!

References

1. Genna, C, Smith L. *Supporting Sucking Skills* (2013): 69.
2. Wilson-Clay B, Hoover, K. *The Breastfeeding Atlas* 2017: 115.
3. The Academy of Breastfeeding Medicine Protocol Committee. *Breastfeeding Medicine*. February 2011;6(1):41-49.
4. Brownell E, Howard CR, Lawrence RA, et al. Delayed onset of lactogenesis II predicts the cessation of any or exclusive breastfeeding. *Journal of Pediatrics 2012;7(6):489-509.*
5. Hill P, Aldag J, Chatterton R, et al. Comparison of milk output between mothers of preterm and term infants: the first 6 weeks after birth. *Journal of Human Lactation* 2005;21(1):22-30.
6. Hill PD, Aldag JC. Predictors of term infant feeding at week 12 postpartum. *Journal of Perinatal and Neonatal Nursing* 2007;21(3):250-255.
7. Genna C, Fram J, Sandora L. *Supporting Sucking Skills* 2013: 338.
8. Hall R, Mercer A, Teasley S, et al. A breastfeeding assessment score to evaluate the risk for cessation of breastfeeding by 7-10 days of age. *Journal of Pediatrics* 2002;141(5):659-664.
9. Parker LA, Sullivan S, Krueger C, Kelechi T, Mueller M. Effect of earl breast milk expression on milk volume and timing of lactogenesis stage II amont mothers of very low birth weight infants: a pilot study. *Journal of Perinatology* 2012;32(2):205-209.
10. Parker LA, Sullivan S, Krueger C, et al. Association of timing of initiation of breastmilk expression on milk volume and timing of lactogenesis stage II among mothers of very low birth weight infants. *Breastfeeding Medicine* 2015;10(2):84-91.
11. Wilson-Clay B, Hoover K. *The Breastfeeding Atlas* 2017: 115.
12. Evans A, Marinelli K, Taylor JS, and The Academy of Breastfeeding Medicine. *Breastfeeding Medicine*. January 2014,9(1):3-8.
13. Wilson-Clay B, Hoover K. *The Breastfeeding Atlas*: 115.
14. United Nations Children's Fund, World Health Organization. Section 1. In: *Baby-Friendly Hospital Initiative: Revised, Updated and Expanded for Integrated Care*. World Health Organization, UNICEF and Wellstart International, Geneva 2009.
15. Joint Commission on Accreditation of Healthcare Organizations. Specifications Manual for Joint Commission National Quality Measures (v2013A1). Measure Information Form PC-05. www.jointcommission.org . Copyright 2012. Accessed February 2018.
16. American Academy of Pediatrics (AAP) Section on Breastfeeding. Breastfeeding and the use of human milk. *Pediatrics* 2012;129(3):e827-841.
17. Flaherman VJ, Gay B, Scott C, Avins A, Lee KA, Newman TB. Randomised trial comparing hand expression with breastpumping for mothers of term newborns feeding poorly. *Arch Dis Child Fetal Neonatal Ed.* 2012 Jan;97(1):F18-23.
18. Genna C, Smith L. *Supporting Sucking Skills* 2013: 71.

19. Kent, J. Volume and frequency of Breastfeedings and Fat Content of Breast Milk Throughout the Day. *Pediatrics* 2006;*117(3).*
20. Dowling D, Thanattherakul W. Nipple confusion, alternative feeding methods, and breastfeeding supplementation: state of the science. *Newborn and Infant Nursing Reviews* 2001;1(4):217-223.
21. Cronenwett L, Stukei T, Kearney M. Single daily bottle use in the early weeks postpartum and breastfeeding outcomes. *Pediatrics* 1992;90(5):760-766.
22. Wilson-Clay B, Hoover K. *The Breastfeeding Atlas* 2017: 46.
23. Ibid, 47.
24. Chen DC, Nommsen-Rivers L, Dewey KG, Lonnerdal B. Stress during labor and delivery and early lactation performance. *American Journal of Clinical Nutrition* 1998;68(2):335-344.
25. Becker GE, Smith HA, Cooney F. Methods of milk expression for lactating women. *Cochrane Databas System Review* 2016;2:CD006170.DOI:10.1002/14651858.
26. Wilson-Clay B, Hoover K. *The Breastfeeding Atlas* 2017: 116-117, 122.
27. Genna C, Fram J, Sandora L. *Supporting Sucking Skills* 2013: 338-344.
28. Ibid, 338.
29. Flaherman V, Hicks K, Cabana M, Lee K. Maternal experience of interactions with providers among mothers with milk supply concern. *Clinical Pediatrics* 2012 Aug;51(8):778-784.
30. Schore, AN. Back to basics: Attachment, affect regulation, and the developing right brain: Linking developmental neuroscience to pediatrics. *Pediatric Review* 2005;26:204-217.
31. Genna C, Smillie C. *Supporting Sucking Skills* 2013: 93.
32. Dunn S, Davies B, McCleary L, Edwards N, Gaboury I. The relationship between vulnerability factors and breastfeeding outcome. *JOGNN* 2006;35(1):87-96.
33. Genna C, Glover R, Wiessinger D. *Supporting Sucking Skills* 2013: 106.
34. Meier, P, et al. Supporting breastfeeding in the neonatal intensive care unit. *Pediatric Clinics of North America* 2013:60(1), 209-226.
35. Flaherman, V, et al (2013). Effect of Early Limited Formula on Duration and Exclusivity of Breastfeeding in At Risk Infants: An RCT. *Pediatrics 131:*1059.
36. Wilson-Clay B, Hoover K. *The Breastfeeding Atlas*: 109.
37. Ibid, 52.
38. Meier, P, et al. Nipple Shields for Preterm Infants: Effect on Milk Transfer and Duration of Breastfeeding. *Journal of Human Lactation* 2000;16(2):106-114.
39. Gerhardsson, E (2014). Breastfeeding Self Efficacy Scale. *Journal of Human Lactation* 2014;30(3): 340-344.
40. Kellams A, Harrel C, Omage S, Gregory C, Rosen-Carole C, and the Academy of Breastfeeding Medicine. *Breastfeeding Medicine*. May 2017,12(4):188-198.
41. Nommsen-Rivers LA, Chantry CJ, Peerson JM, et al. Delayed onset of lactogenesis among first time mothers is related to maternal obesity and factors related to ineffective breastfeeding. *American Journal of Clinical Nutrition* 2010;92(3):574-584.
42. Chapman DJ, Perez-Escamilla R. Identification of risk factors for delayed onset of lactation. *Journal of the American Dietetic Association* 1999;99(4):450-454.
43. Morton J, et al. Combining hand techniques with electric pumping increases milk production in mothers of preterm infants. *Journal of Perinatology* 2009;(29)11:757-764.
44. Gourley G, Kreamer B, Arend R. The effect of diet on feces and jaundice during the first 3 weeks of life. *Gastroenterology* 1992;103:660-661.
45. Gourley G, Kreamer B, Cohnen M. Inhibition of B-glucuronidase by casein hydrosylate formula. *J Pediatr Gastroenterol Nutr* 1997;(25):267-272.
46. Gourley G, Kreamer B, Cohnen M, Kosorok M. Neonatal jaundice and diet. *Arch Pediatr Adolesc Med* 1999;(153):184-188.
47. Kreamer B, Siegel F, Gourley G. A novel inhibitor of B-glucuronidase: L-aspartic acid. *Pediatric Research* 2001 Nov:460-454.
48. Gourley G, Li Z, Kreamer B, Kosorok M. A controlled, randomized, double-blind trial of prophylaxis against jaundice among breastfed newborns. *Pediatrics* 2005 Aug:116(2):385-91.
49. Meier, P, et al (2013). Supporting breastfeeding in the neonatal intensive care unit. *Pediatric Clinics of North America, 60(1)*, 209-226.

50. Woolridge M. The Analysis, Classification, Etiology of Diagnosed Low Milk Output. Conference Presentation, La Leche League of Texas Area Conference, Houston, TX. July 1992.
51. Lussier M, Brownell E, Proulx T, et al. Daily breastmilk volume in mothers of very low birthweight neonates: a repeated-measures randomized trial of hand expression versus electric pump expression. *Breastfeeding Medicine* 2015;10(6):312-317.
52. Hill P, Aldag J, Chatterton R. Initiation and frequency of pumping and milk production in mothers on non-nursing preterm infants. *Journal of Human Lactation* 2001;17(1):9-13.
53. Morton J, Wong R, Hall J, Pang W, Lai C, Lui J, Hartmann P, Rhine W. Combining hand techniques with electric pumping increases the caloric content of milk in mothers of preterm infants. *Journal of Perinatology* 2012;32(10):791-796.
54. Meier P, Furman L, Degenhardt M. Increased lactation for late preterm infants and mothers: Evidence and management strategies to protect breastfeeding. *Journal of Midwifery and Women's Health* 2007;52:579-587.
55. Ramsay, D, et al (2006). Milk Flow Rates Can Be Used to Identify and Investigate Milk Ejection in Women Expressing Breast Milk Using an Electric Breast Pump. *Breastfeeding Medicine 1(1),* 14-23.
56. Genna C, Sandora L. *Supporting Sucking Skills* 2013: 38.
57. Hill, et al (1999). Effects of pumping style on milk production in mothers of non-nursing preterm infants. *Journal of Human Lactation, 15,* 209-215.
58. Hartmann P, Sherriff J, Kent J. Maternal nutrition and the regulation of milk synthesis. *Proceedings of the Nutrition Society* 1995;54:379-389.
59. Neville M, Keller R, Seacat J, et al. Studies in human lactation: milk volumes in lactating women during the onset of lactation and full lactation. *American Journal Clinical Nutrition* 1988;48(6):1375-86.
60. Kent J, Mitoulas L, Cox D, et al. Breast volume and milk production during extended lactation in women. *Experimental Physiology* 1999;84(2):435-447.
61. Meier, P, et al (2004). The Rush mothers' club: breastfeeding interventions for mothers of very low birth weight infants. *Journal of Obstetric, Gynecologic and Neonatal Nursing 33; 164-174.*
62. Stutte P, Bowles B, Morman G. The effects of breast massage on volume and fat content of milk. *Genesis* 1988;10(2):22-25.
63. Mohrbacher N, Kendall-Tackett K. *Breastfeeding Made Simple* 2010: 110-111.
64. Ibid, 136-142.
65. Kent J, Mitoulas L, Cregan M, Geddes D, Larsson M, Doherty D, Hartmann P. Importance of vacuum for milk expression. *Breastfeeding Medicine* 2008 mar;3(1):11-19.
66. Hoban R, Bigger H, Schoeny M, Engstrom J, Meier P, Patel A. Milk Volume a 2 Weeks Predicts Mother's Own Milk Feeding at Neonatal Intensive Care Unit Discharge for Very Low Birthweight Infants. *Breastfeeding Medicine* 2018; 13(2).

Stay Encouraged

Whether you are breastfeeding, breast-milk feeding, and/or formula feeding, I am hopeful that you are breathing deeply and enjoying your baby. If you find yourself holding your breath and worrying about your baby, continue to reach out for further assessment and assistance until you feel that both of you are in a good place. As you settle into your new normal, it will be easier to identify when something is abnormal. In the meantime, it may feel like everything is abnormal. Continue to be patient with yourself and gracious to other mothers whose journey will be different from yours. You're a great mom—and so is she.

Stay encouraged!

Acknowledgements

I am so very grateful for the newborn families who invite me to walk with them through their most vulnerable season of life. To my amazing colleagues and friends, thank you for teaching me, for encouraging me, and for not laughing at me every time I said the book will be done in six months. It takes everybody a decade to write a book, right? Mom and Sara, without you, I'd still just be talking about it. And to my precious family, especially my husband Bo, I love you deeply; you are the reason I press on.

Appendix

Preparing for a Lactation Consult

In the IBCLC office

DO

- Bring items you are currently using or previously used such as bottle, pump, and nipple shield. Pillow and stool will be provided by the consultant.
- Set the appointment as close as possible to a feeding time so that you have a hungry baby and full breasts.
- Bring your support system. Dad and grandmothers are always encouraged to attend. They can help you remember what you hear and put it into action.
- Bring your feeding journal where you have recorded feeding, pumping, pees, and poops.

In your own home

DO

- Decide where you most like to feed. Ask your consultant for suggestions for chairs, stools, or pillows. Have the items you typically use ready and available.
- Invite your support system to come observe, take notes, and help with other children.
- Set the consult appointment as close to a feeding time as possible so that you have a hungry baby and full breasts.
- Fill out your feeding journal where you have recorded feeding, pumping, pees, and poops.

DO NOT

- Clean your house, entertain friends, and bake cookies.
- Get dressed up and plan a full day running around town. Come directly to the appointment and plan to head directly home. You must protect your rest.

Proper Breast Flange Fit

If you answer Yes to any of the following questions, refer to the plan below.

- Do you have any pain when pumping?
- Do you have trouble fully draining your breast?
- Do your nipples have rings, blanching, or skin damage after pumping?

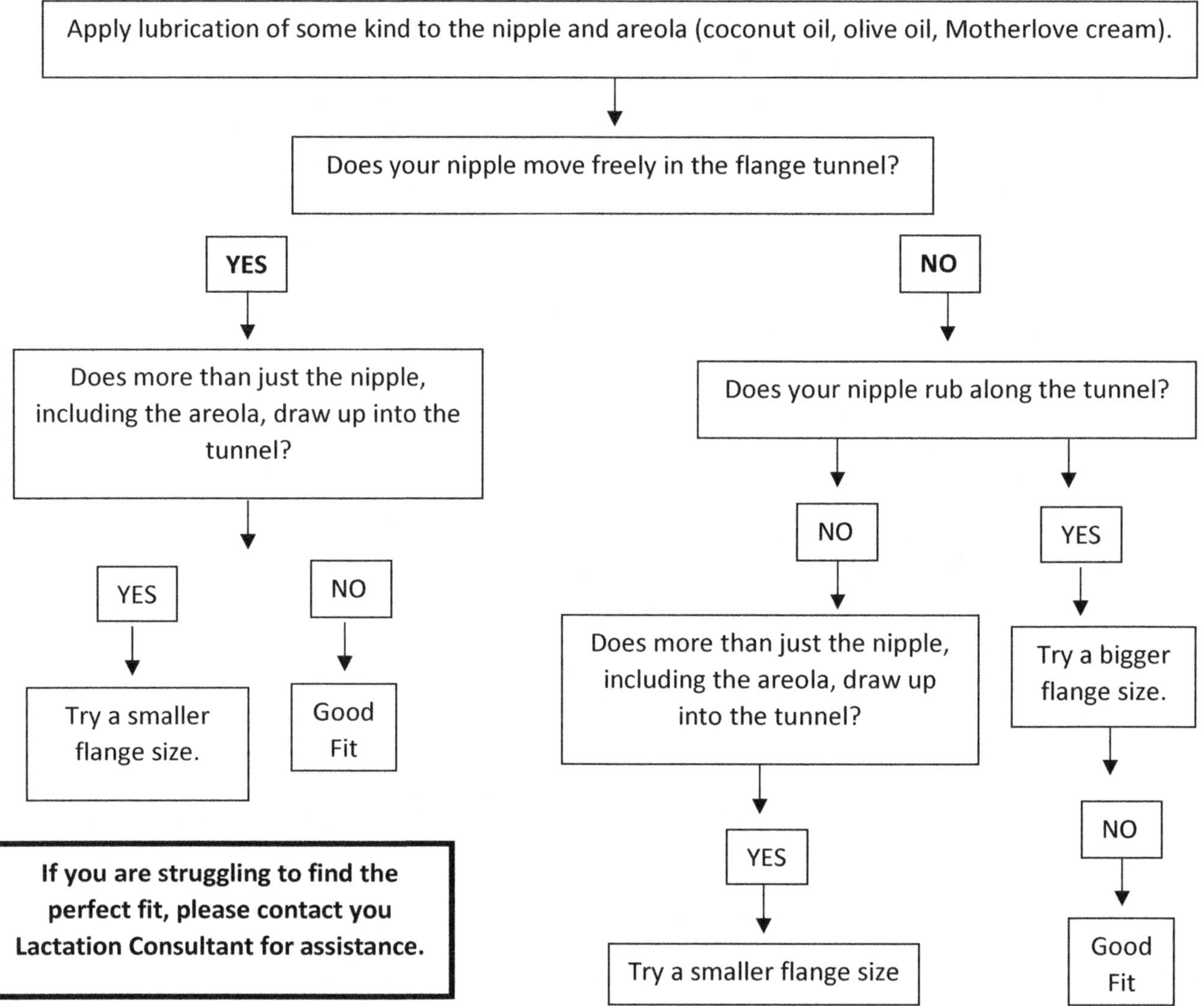

If you are struggling to find the perfect fit, please contact you Lactation Consultant for assistance.

Your breast and nipples will change throughout the breastfeeding or pumping experience.

Recheck your flange size frequently.

Make sure you are not turning the suction above your comfort level.

Breast Flanges come in many sizes depending on the brand of pump you use. Do not mix and match different brands to make a pumping kit. This could decrease the efficiency of your pumping.

Pumping Tips

"Hands On" Pumping Techniques

- http://www.nancymohrbacher.com/articles/2012/6/27/to-pump-more-milk-use-hands-on-pumping.html
- http://newborns.stanford.edu/Breastfeeding/MaxProduction.html

Milk Storage and Handling

- http://kellymom.com/bf/pumpingmoms/milkstorage/milkstorage/
- http://www.medelabreastfeedingus.com/tips-and-solutions/11/collection-and-storage-of-breastmilk
- https://www.cdc.gov/breastfeeding/recommendations/handling_breastmilk.htm

Cleaning Breastpump Parts

- http://www.medelabreastfeedingus.com/products/573/pump-in-style-advanced/faqs
- https://www.cdc.gov/healthywater/pdf/hygeine/breast-pump-fact-sheet.pdf

Breast Pump Suction Troubleshooting

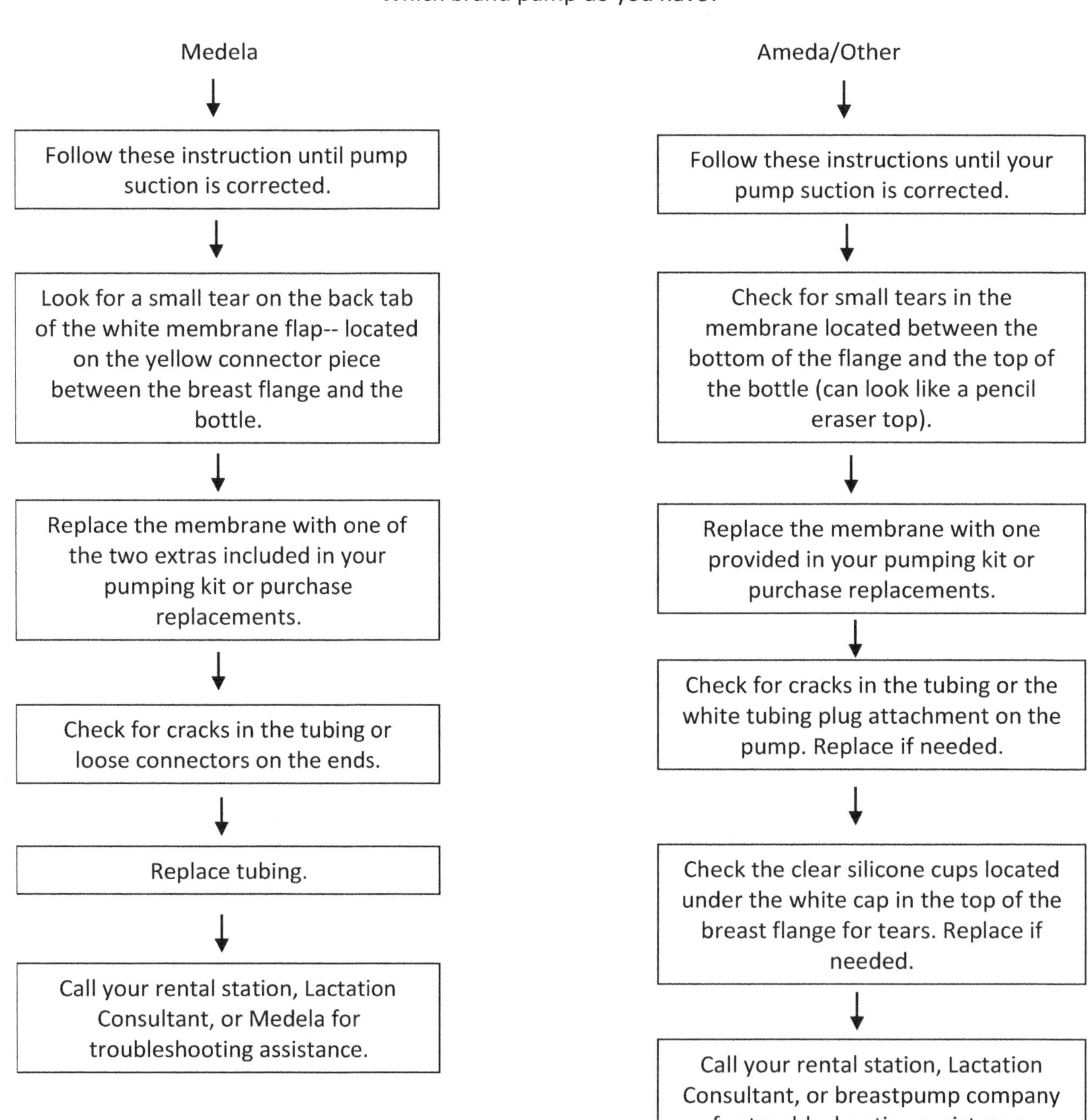

Breast Pump Tubing Condensation

If you see mold, green or black, **THROW AWAY** and replace.

Condensation in Tubing Cloudy /Foggy/Spots
(white or clear)

Make sure you are allowing your tubing to dry fully after each pumping.

Remove the bottles and flanges and allow the pump to run with the tubing attached until the condensation is cleared.

Some white or cloudy water spots are normal and are nothing to be concerned about

Some companies offer instructions on how to sterilize the tubing. Please be sure to follow these instructions EXACTLY and only when necessary. Incorrect cleaning can result in the tubing melting, which causes connector ends to become loose.

Milk Overflow

Make sure the pump's valve and membrane are moving freely during your pumping session.

Be sure to remove valve and wash between each pumping. Valve must have adequate movement.

If you are a mom with a "faster" let down, you will find that you may need to release the suction at your breast more frequently to allow the pump time to catch up. There is only a certain amount of milk that will fit between the flange and bottle without overflow.

If milk overflows into the tubing, follow the cleaning instructions from breastpump company. Remove the milk and then attach the tubing to the pump motor. Allow it to run and dry out the tubing.

Diaper Rash Suggestions

The inside of a baby's diaper is dark, warm, and moist – a germ's paradise.

To limit growth of germs and heal skin, it is helpful to expose diaper rash to light, a little cool air, and complete drying of skin prior to applying ointment.

1. When at home, use paper towels with warm water to **rinse and pat the diaper area**. Wiping motions can irritate tender skin. Baby wipes can leave a film on the skin.

2. When out of the house, baby wipes will most likely be necessary. Avoid excessive pressure on the skin when wiping.

3. After rinsing, allow bottom to air dry. You can flip baby over on his stomach for a few minutes. **Avoid applying diaper rash treatment to wet skin as this may make it worse**.

4. Apply diaper rash treatment to a **dry bottom**. Ointments, like A&D™ ointment, Vaseline™, Aquaphor™, or perhaps a diaper ointment compounded by your local pharmacy, serve as a barrier. They are also a soothing emollient to the skin. Zinc oxide-based treatments, on the other hand, are thick and sticky barriers. They must be removed with each diaper change, which requires repeated wiping of tender skin.

5. If the rash persists more than 72 hours, or if any other symptoms occur, call to make an appointment with your pediatrician to examine your baby.

What are the Priorities?

Mom **IS NOT** experiencing pain AND baby has great weight gain

USE LEFT PAGE/SIDE OF CHART

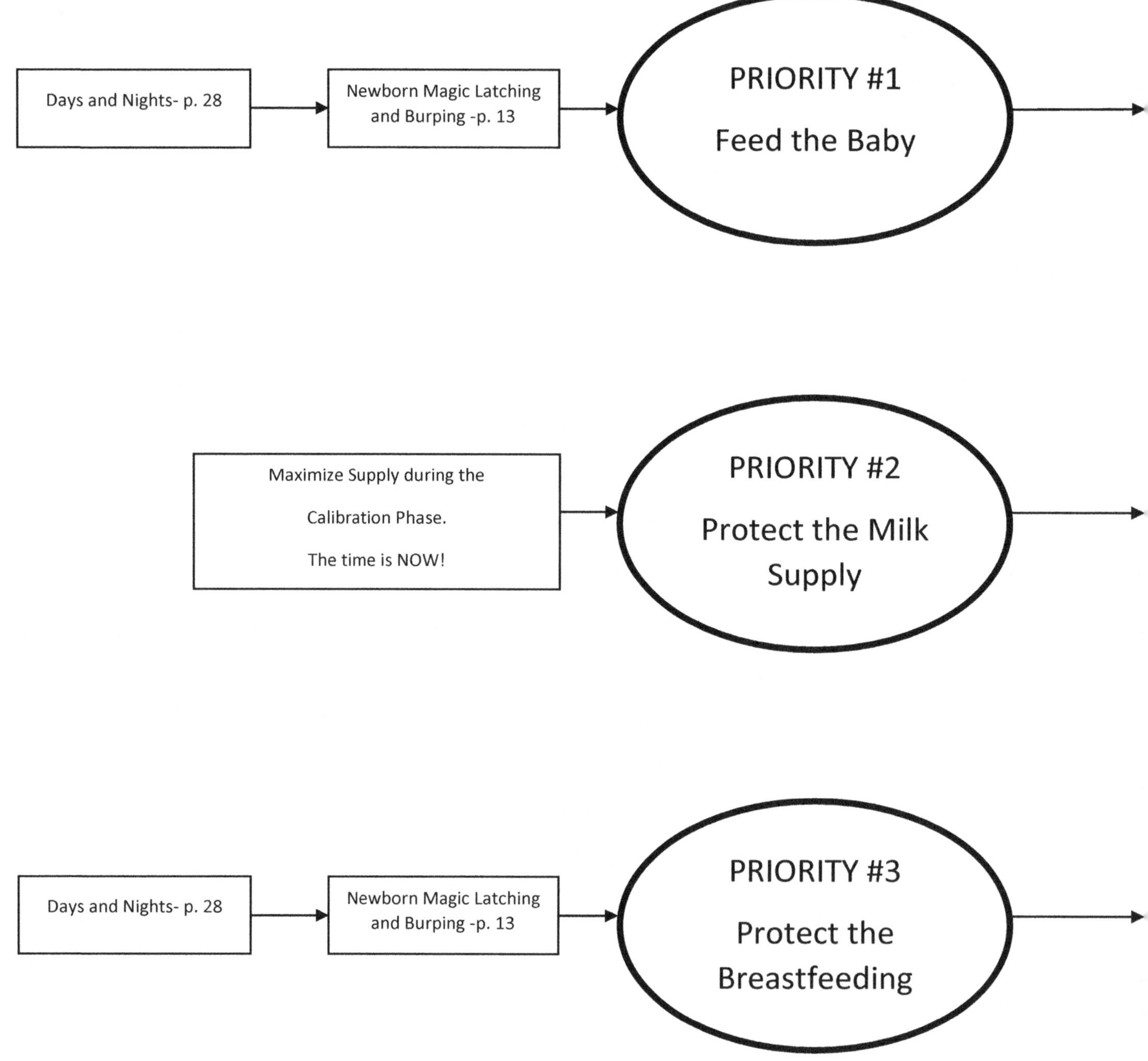

What are the Priorities?

Mom **IS experiencing pain** AND/OR baby is not yet gaining weight

USE RIGHT PAGE/SIDE OF CHART

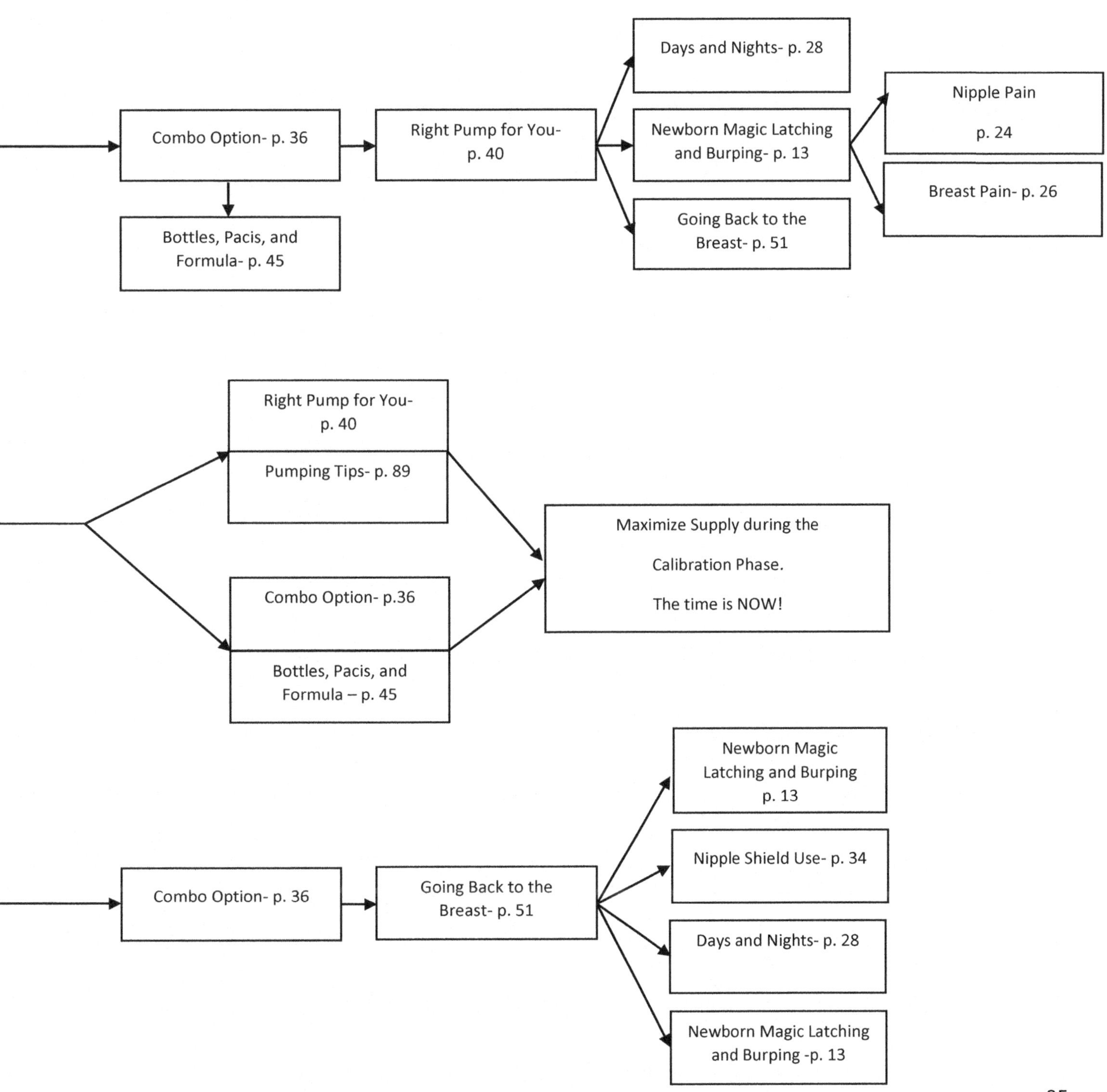

Milk Journals

Breastmilk Storage Guidelines

https://www.cdc.gov/breastfeeding/recommendations/handling_breastmilk.htm

http://kellymom.com/bf/pumpingmoms/milkstorage/milkstorage/

http://www.medelabreastfeedingus.com/tips-and-solutions/11/collection-and-storage-of-breastmilk

Using the Milk Journals

- **There are two different sets of journals**. The first set, the **Combination** Journals on pages 99-113 are for moms who are breastfeeding and just want to track their progress. It is also for moms who are doing a combination of breastfeeding plus extra milk in bottles. The second set, the **Exclusively Pumping** Journals on pages 116-129 are for moms who are exclusively pumping and offering milk in bottles only. Each set includes 14 separate pages that correlate with the baby's day of age. See ***example*** on next page, which is Day 3 of age, for a baby feeding from the breast and taking extra milk.
- **Each set of journals is divided into the phases** of your breastfeeding journey: *Initiating Your Milk Supply*, *Growing Your Milk Supply*, and *Maintaining Your Milk Supply.* Dr. Paula Meier and her team at Rush University Medical Center in Chicago developed this approach to help mothers whose babies need extra milk to achieve their short and long-term breastfeeding goals (Meier 2016).
- **The journals provide a central place to gather information that will put your mind at ease**. You will be able to see that your baby is getting enough milk and that you are making enough milk. You can also make notes and write down questions you have for your health care providers. There's also a place to record baby's weight if you see your pediatrician or IBCLC that day. It is ok if you need to shift from one set of journals to the other during this time, depending on your feeding situation.
- **Each day is divided into boxes to keep track of different aspects of your feeding routine**. In the combination journals, there is an area to identify *how* you fed your baby at that particular feeding time. You can use a "**B**" for breastfeeding, "**PM**" for pumped milk, "**IF**" for infant formula, or a combination. See ***example*** on the next page. When and if exclusively pumping moms are ready to begin the transition back to the breast, you can start using the Combination journals.
- **Specific goals for each day are included**. In the exclusive pumping journals, milk production goals are included in the notes section. In both sets of journals, the daily goal for feedings, pumpings, and baby's poops are indicated by a box with a **dashed border**. If your baby is not eating or pooping enough times, **contact your pediatrician and lactation consultant**.
- **The journals use both milliliters and ounces**. Feel free to use what works best for you. The precise conversion of 1 ounce (oz) is 28.3 milliliters (ml). In most settings, it is rounded up to 1 oz = 30 ml.
- **The general goal for each feeding session is soft breasts and a happy baby**. In the first few days, your breasts may be soft, but the baby isn't happy. Due to the very rich but limited volume of colostrum, this can be normal. However, if your baby has lost excessive weight, your pediatrician may recommend that you start pumping and feeding extra milk to the baby. Conversely, after your mature milk volume starts to increase, your breasts may be painfully full and the baby is happy before you are soft. Use the **Breast Pain** care plan on page 26 and pump just until your breasts are comfortable. It's ok if you don't get much out; just stay comfortable. Note: if you have been advised not to pump, that advice is not appropriate in this situation. Keeping your breasts soft and drained in the first two weeks is essential to establishing a full supply and avoiding breast infection. **If you develop an oversupply, that can be resolved in time; however, undersupply sometimes cannot**. See **Priorities** on page 69 and **Right Pump for You** on page 40.
- **If your baby is already past day 14 of age**, you can photocopy the day 14 journal (page 113 or 129) as many times as needed for your personal use. Note: Babies older than 2 weeks may be able to eat fewer than 8 times daily and still gain weight well. Likewise, some moms can pump less than 8 times daily and maintain a full milk supply (900+ ml or 30 oz). Consult with your IBCLC as you are transitioning through the different phases of lactation.

Reference

Meier PP, et al. Which Breast Pump for Which Mother: An Evidence- Based Approach to Individualizing Breast Pump Technology. *J Perinatology 2016.*

Combination Journal

Phase One- Initiating Your Milk Supply

DAY 3 of Age

EXAMPLE

What **did you feed your baby at this feeding?**

B-Breastfeeding PM- Pumped Milk IF- Infant Formula

If extra milk is needed, *how much* did the baby take in mililiters?

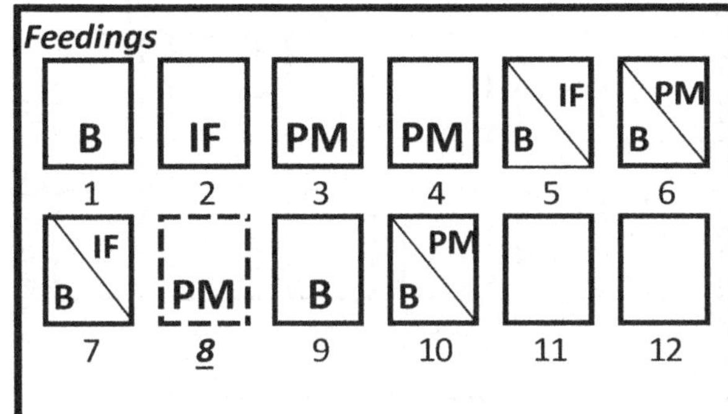

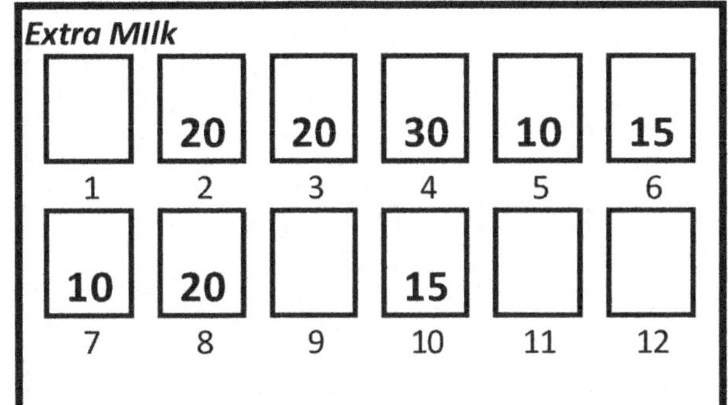

EXAMPLE

If hand expresseion and pumping is needed, *how many* milliliters did you get from both breasts combined?

How much *total* milk did you pump *today*?

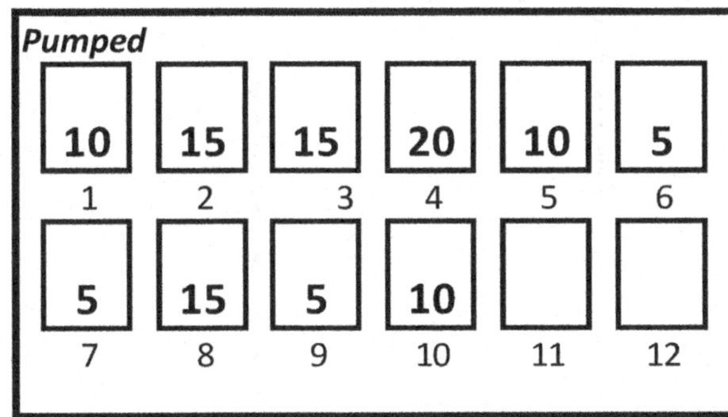

How many times did the baby poop today?

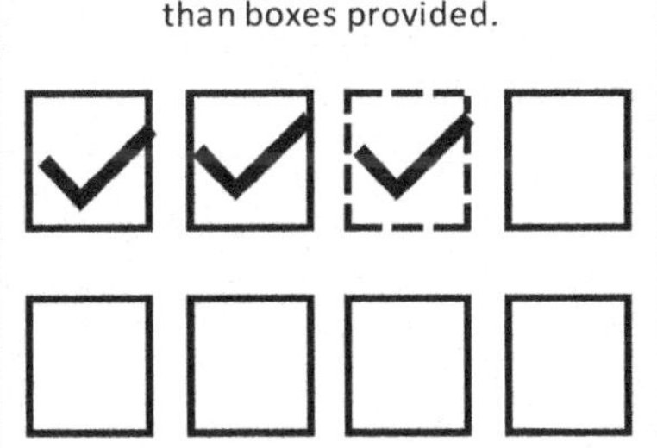

Goal of 3 or more today

Helpful tips for today

* You may notice your breasts feeling more full today.

*If you are uncomfortably full, see **Breast Pain** page 26.

* If your nipples are tender, see **Nipple Pain** page 24.

Questions and Notes:

Baby's weight today:__________

EXAMPLE

Combination Journal

Phase One- Initiating Your Milk Supply

DAY 1 of Age

What **did you feed your baby at this feeding?**

B-Breastfeeding PM- Pumped Milk IF- Infant Formula

If extra milk is needed, *how much* did the baby take in milliliters?

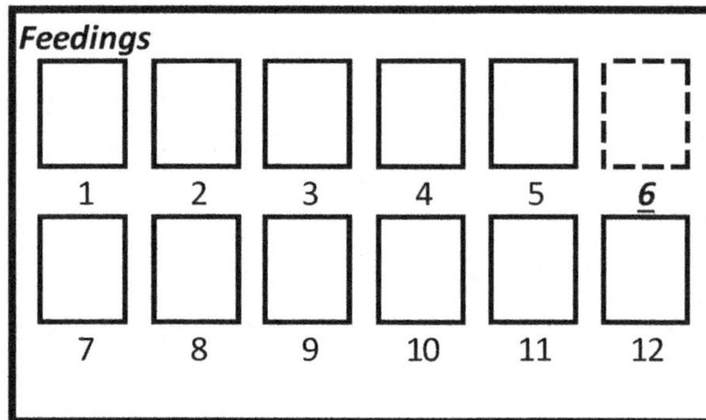

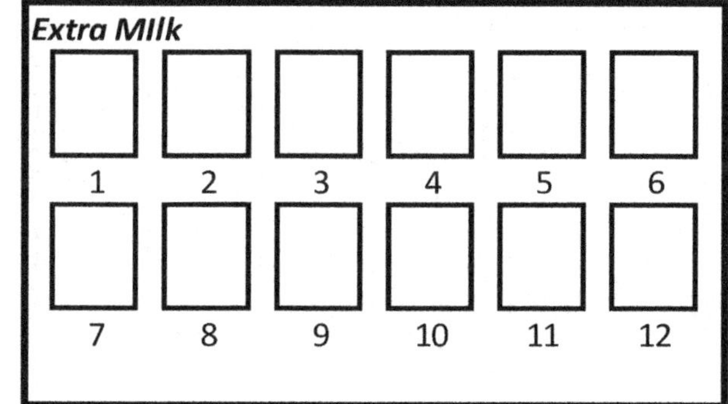

If hand expression and pumping is needed, *how many* milliliters did you get from both breasts combined?

How much milk *total* did you pump *today* ?

Pumped

1 2 3 4 5 6

7 8 9 10 11 12

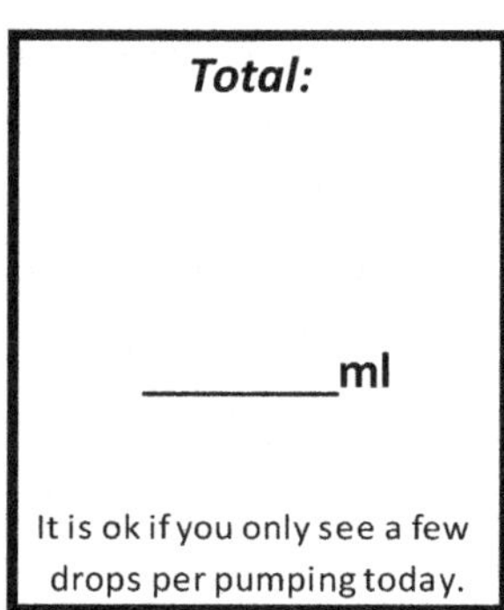

How many times did the baby poop today?

Poops

It is ok if you have more poops than boxes provided.

Goal of 1 or more today

Helpful tips for today

*Your baby may sleep between feedings today. Do a lot of skin to skin contact.

* If your baby is not nursing well yet, http://newborns.stanford.edu/Breastfeeding/HandExpression.html

Questions and Notes:

Baby's weight today:__________

Combination Journal

Phase One- Initiating Your Milk Supply

DAY 2 of Age

What **did you feed your baby at this feeding?**

B-Breastfeeding PM- Pumped Milk IF- Infant Formula

If extra milk is needed, *how much* did the baby take in milliliters?

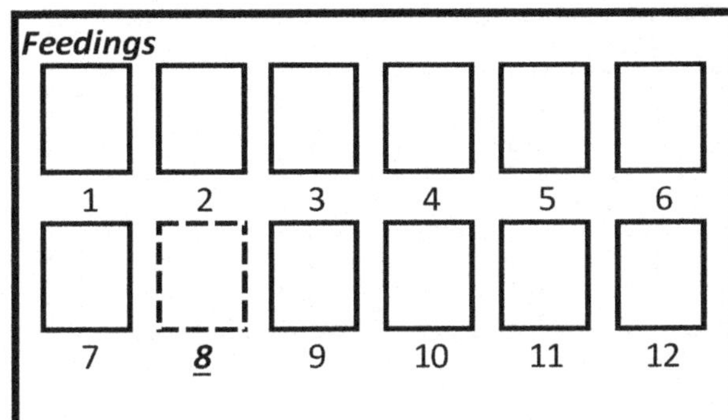

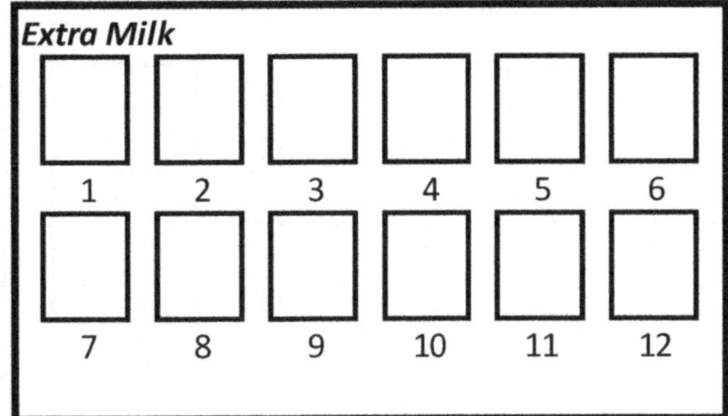

If hand expression and pumping is needed, *how many* milliliters did you get from both breasts combined?

Pumped

1	2	3	4	5	6
7	8	9	10	11	12

How much *total* milk did you pump *today* ?

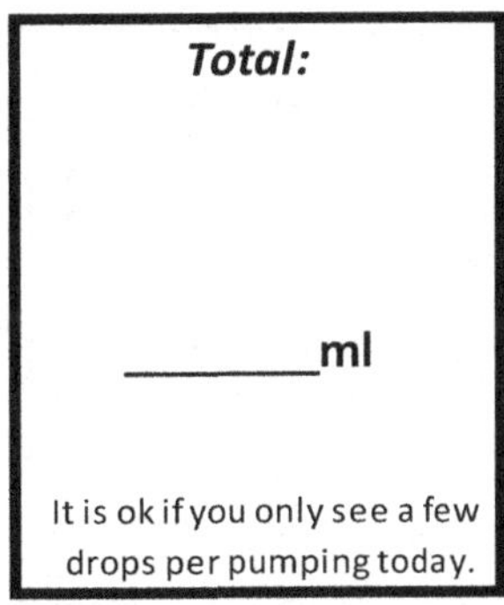

How many times did the baby poop today?

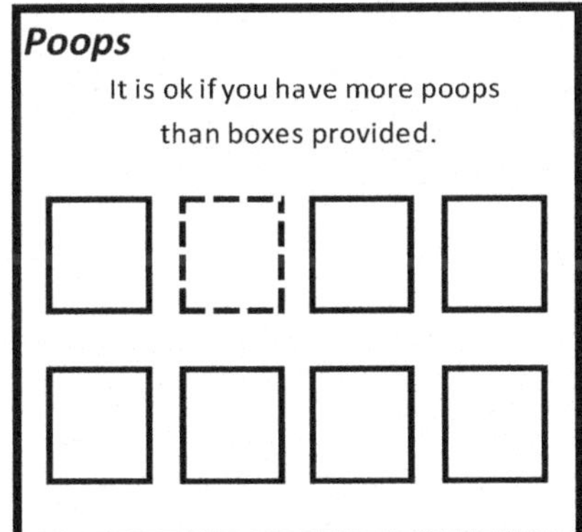

Goal of 2 or more today

Helpful tips for today

*Limit your visitors as much as possible today so that you can have privacy for skin to skin and frequent nursing and/or hand express your milk. See **Days and Nights** page 28.

* If your son is circumcised today, he may not nurse as actively for a few hours after the procedure.

*Your baby may nurse more frequently tonight.

Quetions and Notes:

Baby's weight today:__________

Combination Journal

Phase One- Initiating Your Milk Supply

DAY 3 of Age

What **did you feed your baby at this feeding?**

B-Breastfeeding PM- Pumped Milk IF- Infant Formula

If extra milk is needed, *how much* did the baby take in milliliters?

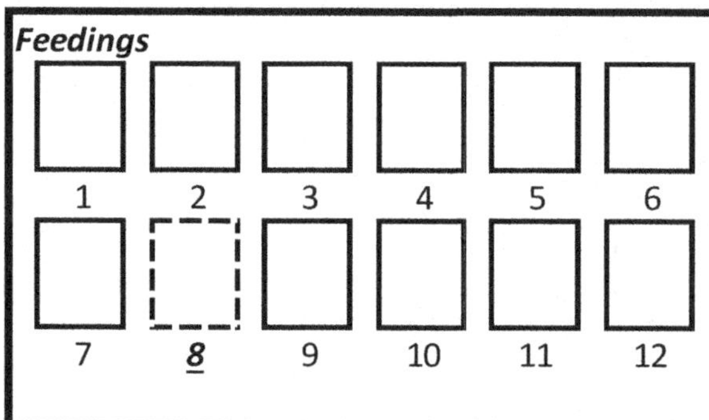

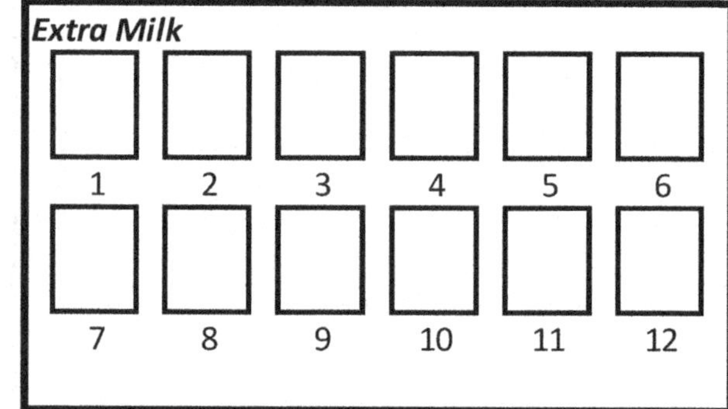

If hand expession and pumping is needed, *how many* milliliters did you get from both breasts combined?

How much *total* milk did you pump *today* ?

Pumped

1 2 3 4 5 6

7 8 9 10 11 12

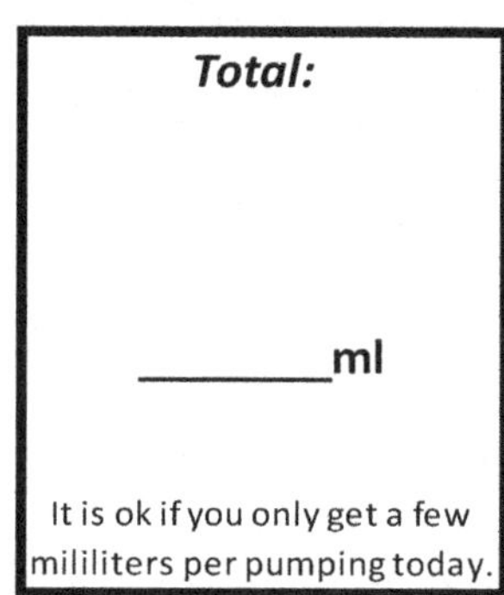

How many times did the baby poop today?

Poops

It is ok if you have more poops than boxes provided.

Goal of 3 or more today

Helpful tips for today

* You may notice your breasts feeling more full today.

*If you are uncomfortably full, see **Breast Pain** page 26.

* If your nipples are tender see, **Nipple Pain** page 24.

Questions and Notes:

Baby's weight today:__________

Combination Journal

Phase One- Initiating Your Milk Supply

DAY 4 of Age

What **did you feed your baby at this feeding?**

B-Breastfeeding PM- Pumped Milk IF- Infant Formula

If extra milk is needed, ***how much*** **did the baby take in milliliters?**

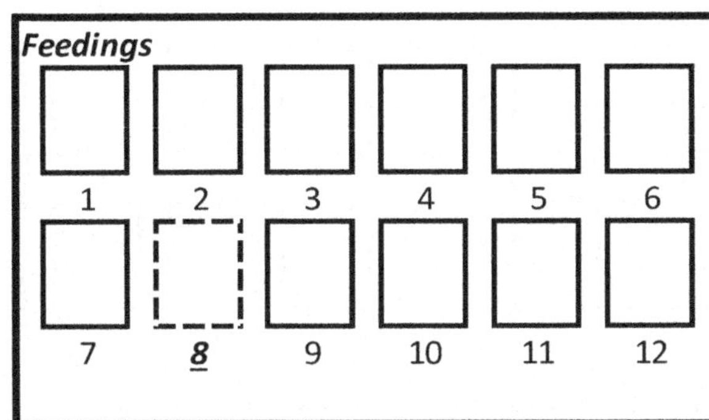

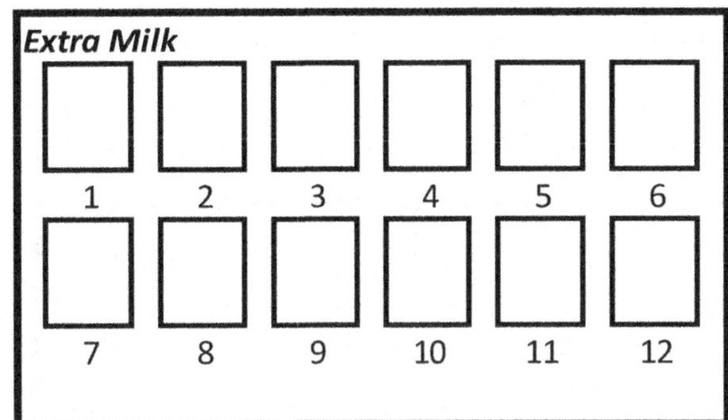

If hand expession and pumping is needed, ***how many*** **milliliters did you get from both breasts combined?**

Pumped

1 2 3 4 5 6

7 8 9 10 11 12

How much ***total*** **milk did you pump** ***today*****?**

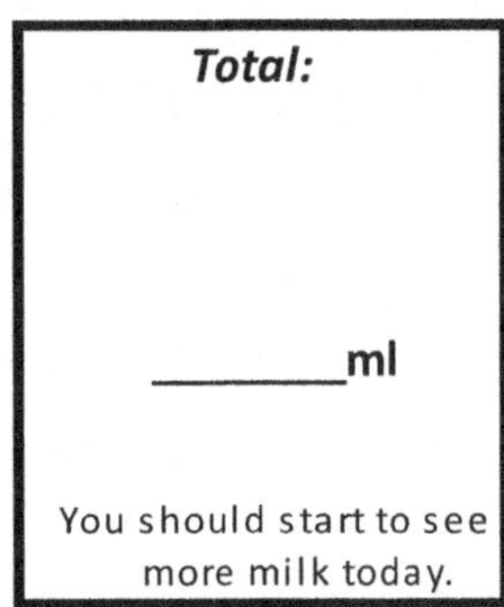

How many times did the baby poop today?

Poops

It is ok if you have more poops than boxes provided.

Goal of 3 or more today

Helpful tips for today

* Your baby may be more jaundiced today. See **Breastfeeding During Jaundice** page 31.

*If your pediatrician recommends extra milk, see **Combination Feeding Option** page 36 and **Bottles, Pacis and Formula** page 45.

Questions and Notes:

Baby's weight today:__________

Combination Journal

Phase Two- Establishing Your Full Milk Supply

DAY 5 of Age

***What* did you feed your baby at this feeding?**

B-Breastfeeding PM- Pumped Milk IF- Infant Formula

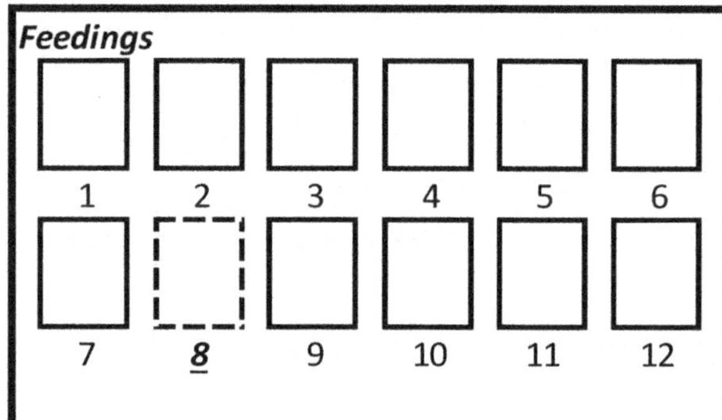

If extra milk is needed, *how much* did the baby take in ounces?

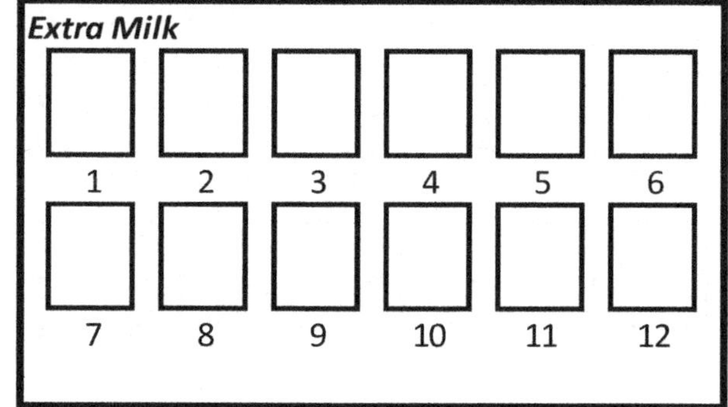

If pumping is needed, *how many milliliters* did you get from both breasts combined?

Pumped

1	2	3	4	5	6
7	8	9	10	11	12

How much *total* milk did you pump *today*?

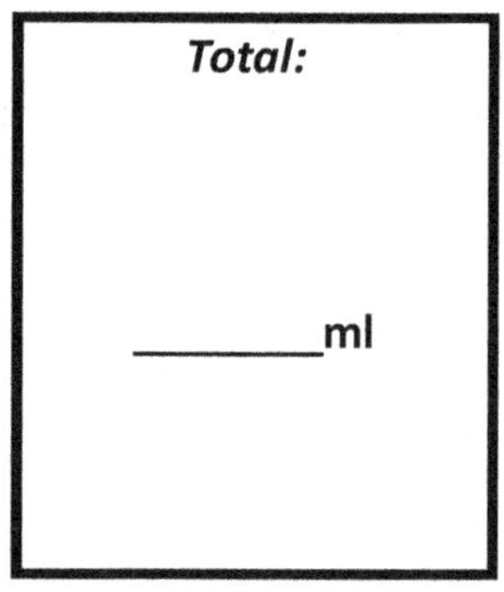

How many times did the baby poop today?

Poops

It is ok if you have more poops than boxes provided.

Goal of 4 or more today

Helpful tips for today

*If your pump isn't draining/softening your breasts,
See **Right Pump for You** page 40.

*If you are still needing to supplement your baby with formula, meet with your IBCLC asap.

Questions and Notes:

Baby's weight today:__________

Combination Journal

Phase Two- Growing Your Full Milk Supply

DAY 6 of Age

What **did you feed your baby at this feeding?**

B-Breastfeeding PM- Pumped Milk IF- Infant Formula

If extra milk is needed, *how much* did the baby take in milliliters?

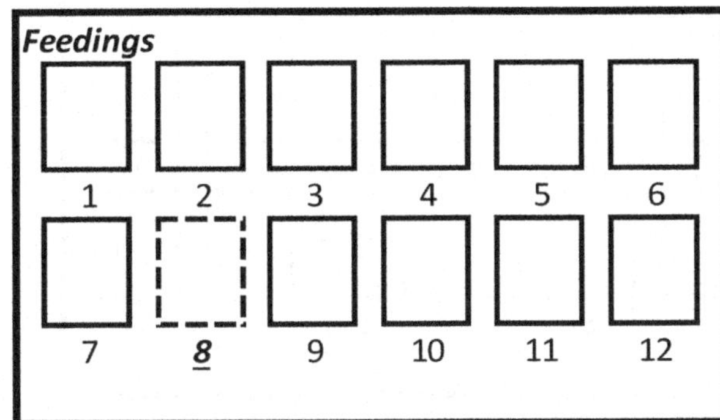

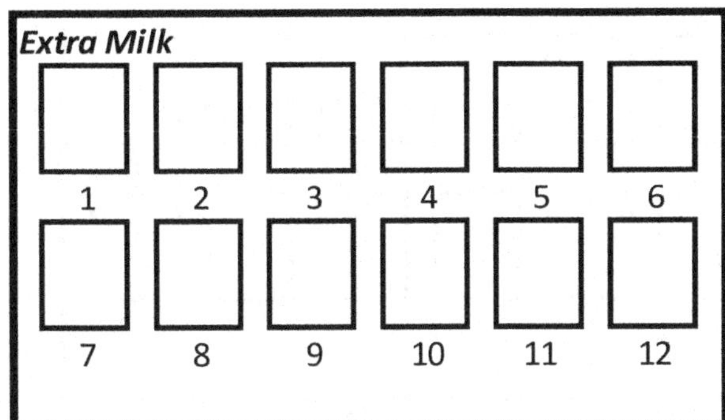

If pumping is needed, *how many milliliters* did you get from both breasts combined?

How much *total* milk did you pump *today* ?

Pumped

1	2	3	4	5	6
7	8	9	10	11	12

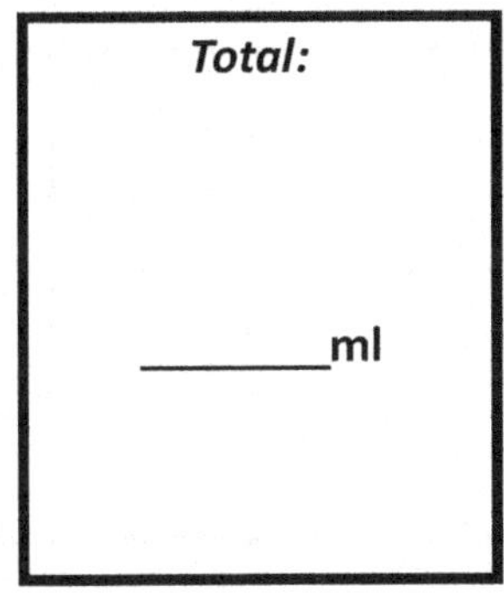

How many times did the baby poop today?

Poops

It is ok if you have more poops than boxes provided.

Goal of 4 or more today

Helpful tips for today

*If you are still experiencing nipple pain, see **Nipple Shield Use** page 34 and see your IBCLC as soon as possible.

*It is ok if you need to pump. See **Combination Feeding Option** page 36

.* Your baby may eat more frequently tonight.

* It doesn't matter how much you are producing.
Just make sure your breasts are comfortable after pumping.

Questions and Notes:

Baby's weight today:_________

Combination Journal

Phase Two- Growing Your Full Milk Supply

DAY 7 of Age

What **did you feed your baby at this feeding?**

B-Breastfeeding PM- Pumped Milk IF- Infant Formula

If extra milk is needed, *how much* did the baby take in milliliters?

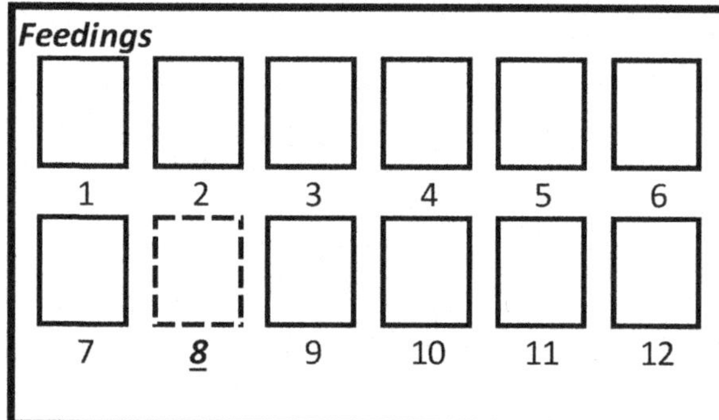

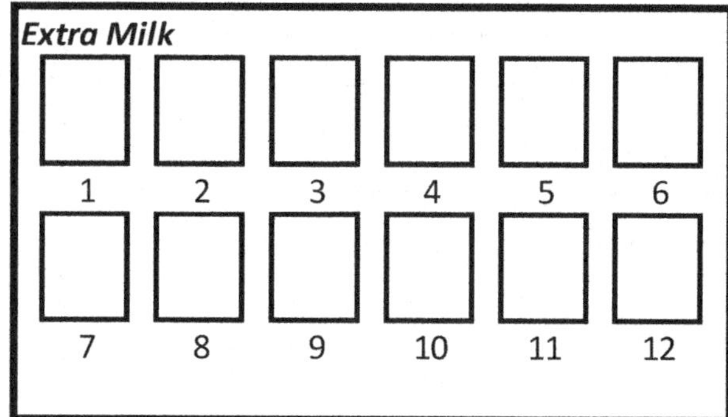

If pumping is needed, *how many milliliters* did you get from both breasts combined?

How much *total* milk did you pump *today* ?

Pumped

1 2 3 4 5 6

7 8 9 10 11 12

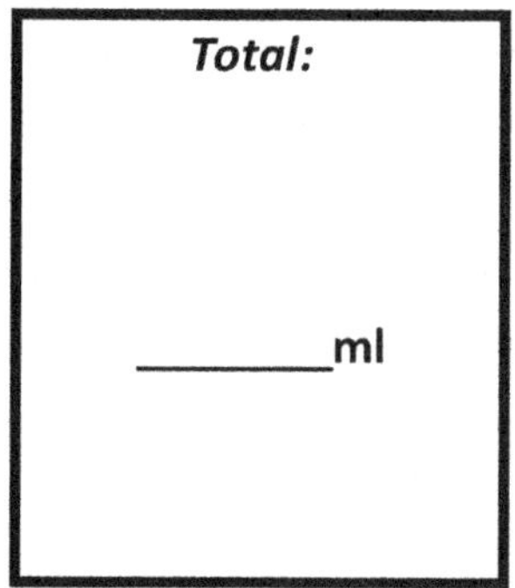

How many times did the baby poop today?

Poops

It is ok if you have more poops than boxes provided.

Goal of 4 or more today

Helpful tips for today

*If you are still struggling with your baby's latch, make an appointment with your IBCLC.

* If your baby is starting to spit up a little, stop to burp him more often. See **Magic Newborn Latch and Burping** page 13 and 21.

Questions and Notes:

Baby's weight today:__________

Combination Journal

Phase Two- Growing Your Full Milk Supply

DAY 8 of Age

What **did you feed your baby at this feeding?**

B-Breastfeeding PM- Pumped Milk IF- Infant Formula

If extra milk is needed, *how much* did the baby take in mililiters?

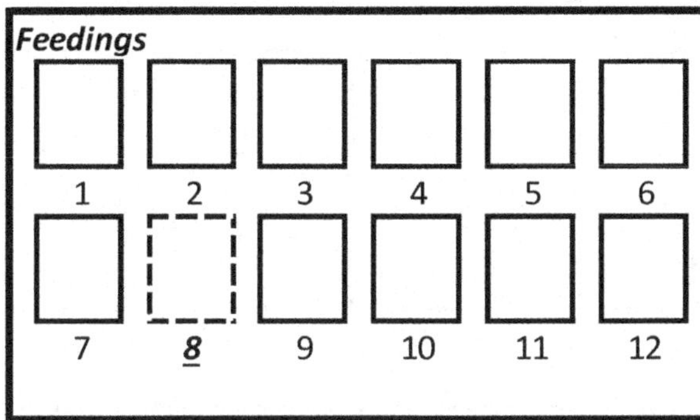

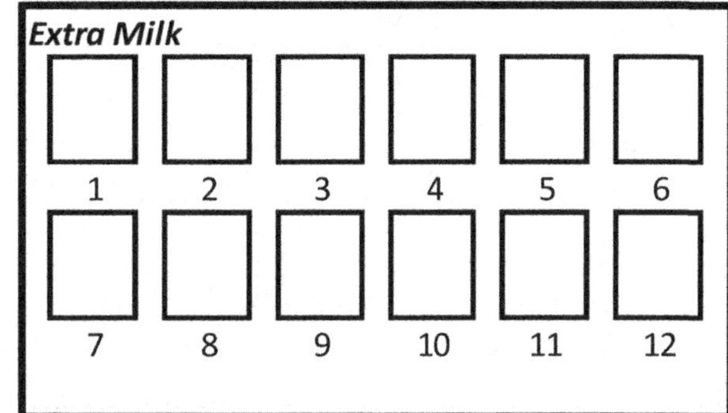

If pumping is needed, *how many milliliters* did you get from both breasts combined?

How much *total* milk did you pump *today* ?

Pumped

1 2 3 4 5 6

7 8 9 10 11 12

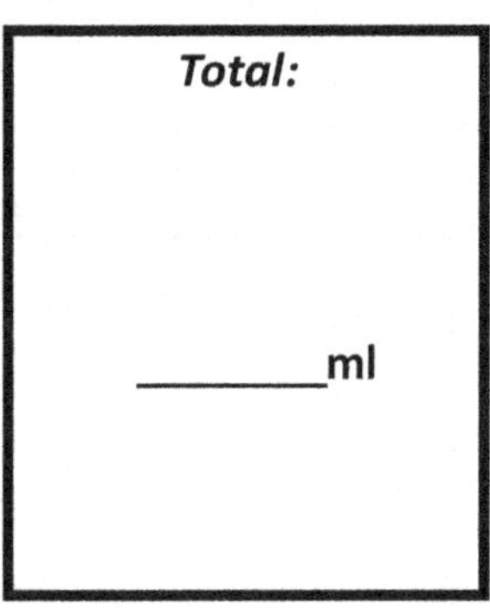

How many times did the baby poop today?

Poops

It is ok if you have more poops than boxes provided.

Goal of 4 or more today

Helpful tips for today

* You may notice that your baby is eating a little more today. The first growth spurt is typically 7-9 days of age.

* If your breast or nipples hurt, see **Nipple Pain** page 24 and **Breast Pain** page 26.

Questions and Notes:

Baby's weight today:__________

Combination Journal

Phase Three- Maintining Your Full Milk Supply

DAY 9 of Age

What did you feed your baby at this feeding?

B-Breastfeeding PM- Pumped Milk IF- Infant Formula

If extra milk is needed, *how much* did the baby take in milliliters?

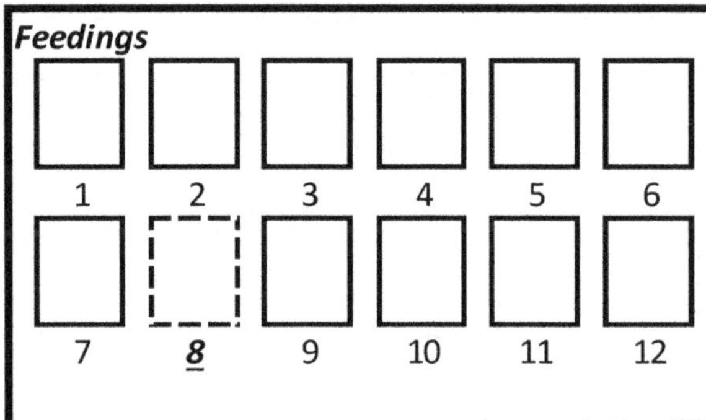

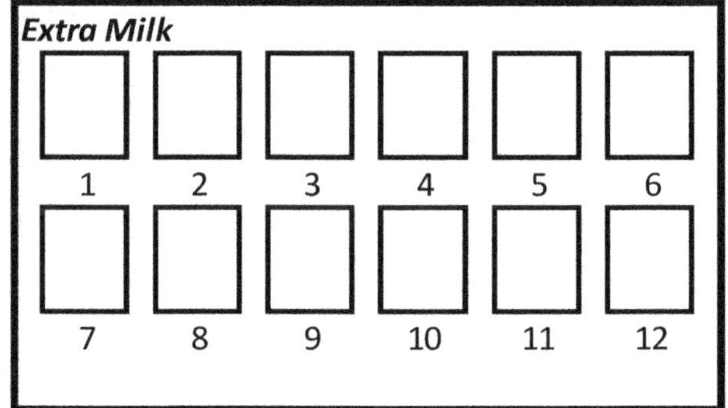

If pumping is needed, *how many milliliters* did you get from both breasts combined?

How much *total* milk did you pump *today* ?

Pumped

1 2 3 4 5 6

7 8 9 10 11 12

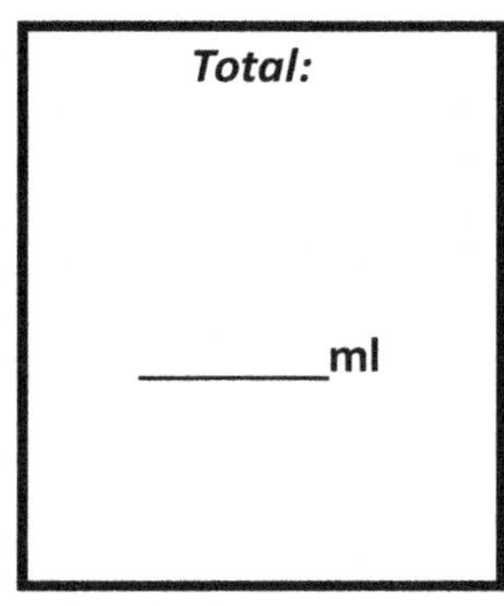

How many times did the baby poop today?

Poops

It is ok if you have more poops than boxes provided.

Goal of 4 or more today

Helpful tips for today

* Hang in there; it gets easier!

* Meet with your IBCLC if your nipples or breasts hurt.

Questions and Notes:

Baby's weight today:__________

Combination Journal

Phase Three- Maintining Your Full Milk Supply

DAY 10 of Age

What **did you feed your baby at this feeding?**

B-Breastfeeding PM- Pumped Milk IF- Infant Formula

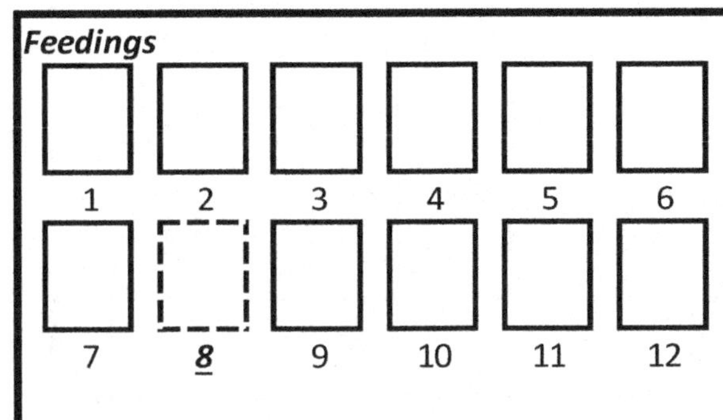

If extra milk is needed, *how much* did the baby take in milliliters?

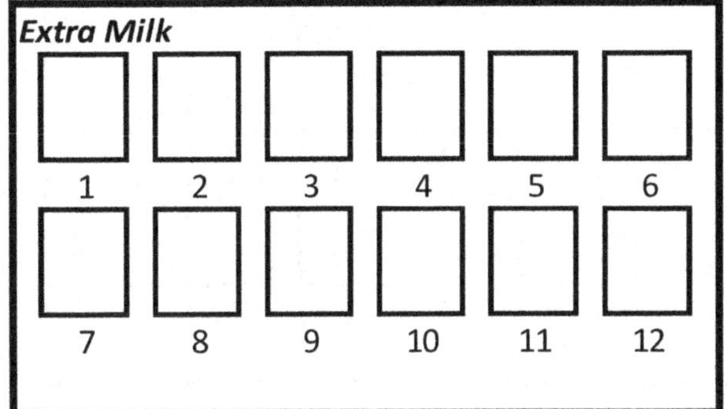

If pumping is needed, *how many milliliters* did you get from both breasts combined?

Pumped

1 2 3 4 5 6

7 8 9 10 11 12

How much *total* milk did you pump *today* ?

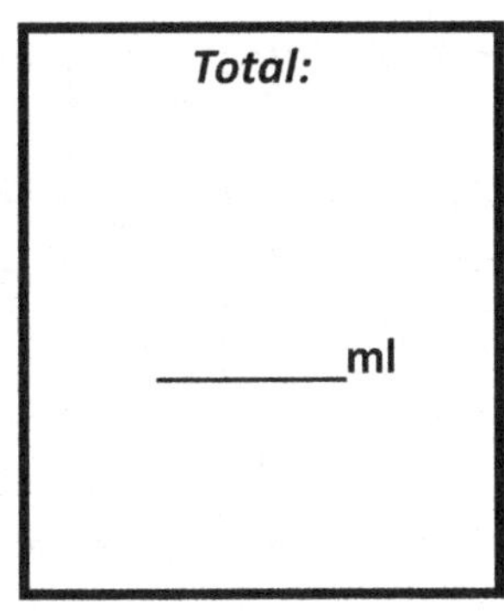

How many times did the baby poop today?

Poops

It is ok if you have more poops than boxes provided.

Goal of 4 or more today

Helpful tips for today

* Remember to keep protecting rest for you and your baby. See **Days and Nights** page 28.

* If your baby still needs supplementation with infant formula, contact your IBCLC.

Questions and Notes:

Baby's weight today:__________

Combination Journal

Phase Three- Maintaining Your Full Milk Supply

DAY 11 of Age

What **did you feed your baby at this feeding?**

B-Breastfeeding PM- Pumped Milk IF- Infant Formula

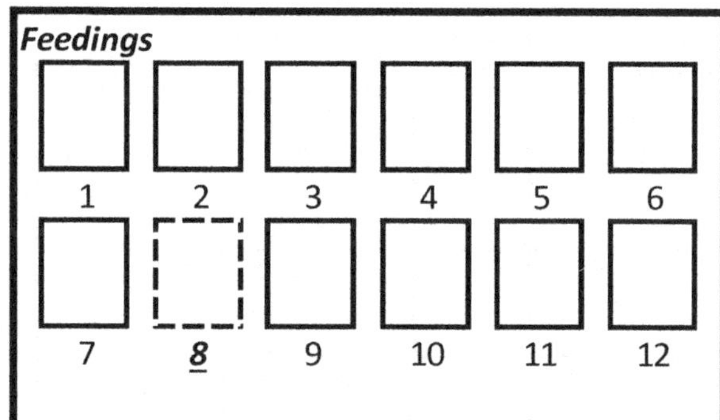

If extra milk is needed, ***how much*** **did the baby take in mililiters?**

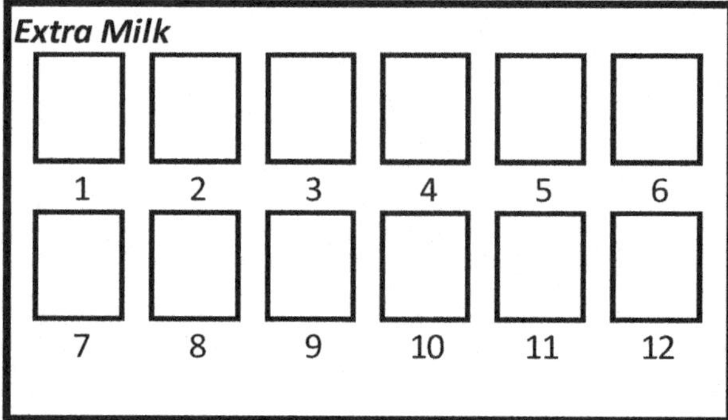

If pumping is needed, ***how many milliliters*** **did you get from both breasts combined?**

Pumped

1	2	3	4	5	6
7	8	9	10	11	12

How much ***total*** **milk did you pump** ***today*****?**

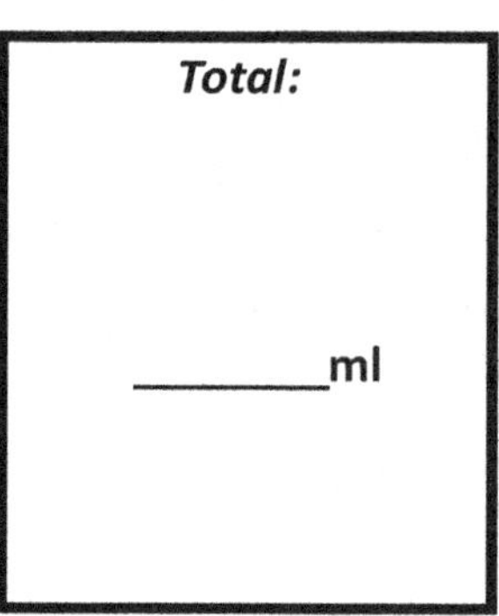

How many times did the baby poop today?

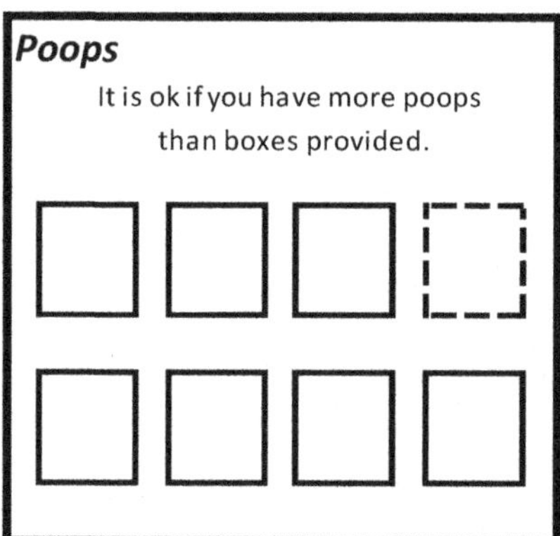

Goal of 4 or more today

Helpful tips for today

* Some babies poop a little at every feed at this age. If he has a diaper rash, see **Diaper Rash** page 92.

* If you are feeling physically or emotionally overwhelmed, reach out to a family member or friend for support. Don't hesitate to call and talk with your OB.

Questions and Notes:

Baby's weight today:__________

Combination Journal

Phase Tree- Maintaining Your Full Milk Supply

DAY 12 of Age

What **did you feed your baby at this feeding?**

B-Breastfeeding PM- Pumped Milk IF- Infant Formula

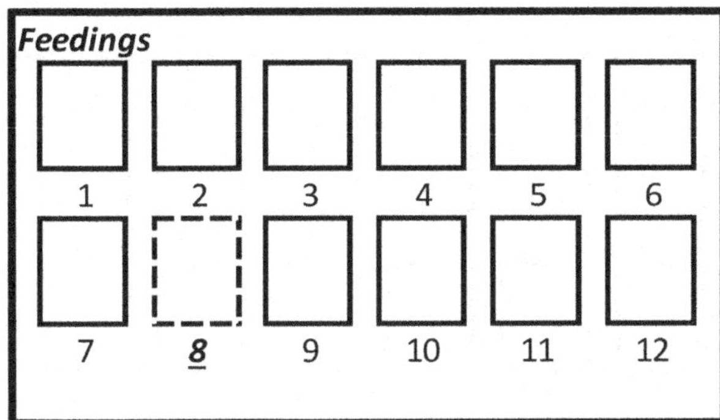

If extra milk is needed, *how much* did the baby take in milliliters?

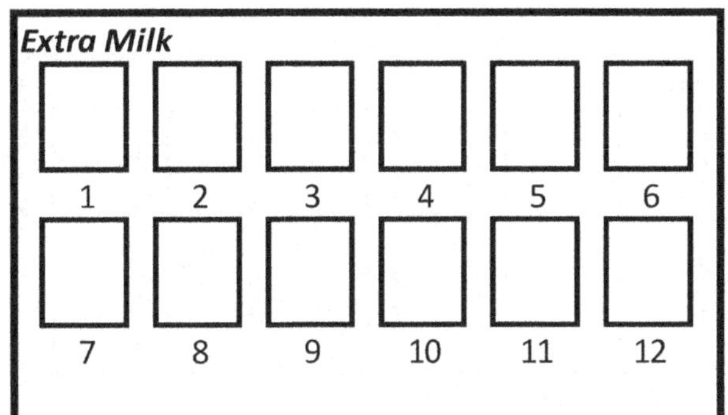

If pumping is needed, *how many milliliters* did you get from both breasts combined?

Pumps

1 2 3 4 5 6

7 8 9 10 11 12

How much *total* milk did you pump *today*?

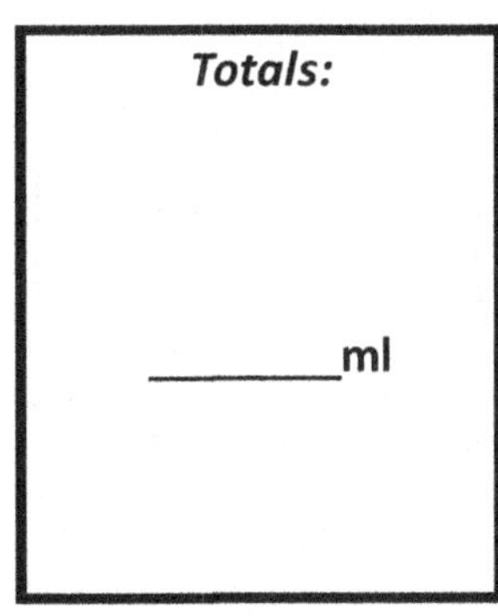

How many times did the baby poop today?

Poops

It is ok if you have more poops than boxes provided.

Goal of 4 or more today

Helpful tips for today

* If you have extra milk in the refrigerator, go ahead and freeze that milk. More info on milk storage on page 89.

* If you are barely keeping up with your baby, check in with your IBCLC.

Questions and Notes:

Baby's weight today:__________

Combination Journal

Phase Three- Maintining Your Full Milk Supply

DAY 13 of Age

What **did you feed your baby at this feeding?**

B-Breastfeeding PM- Pumped Milk IF- Infant Formula

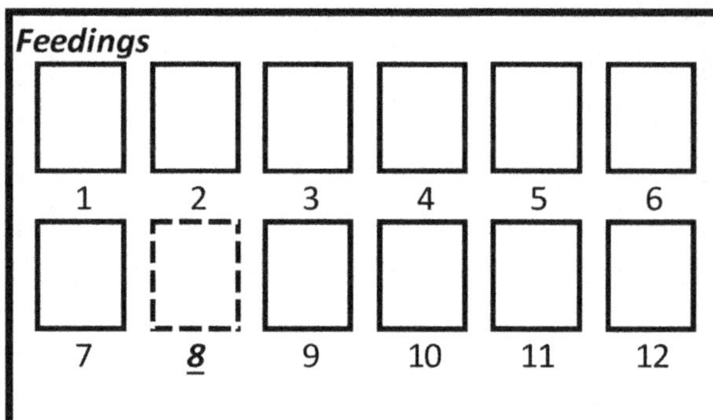

If extra milk is needed, *how much* did the baby take in milliliters?

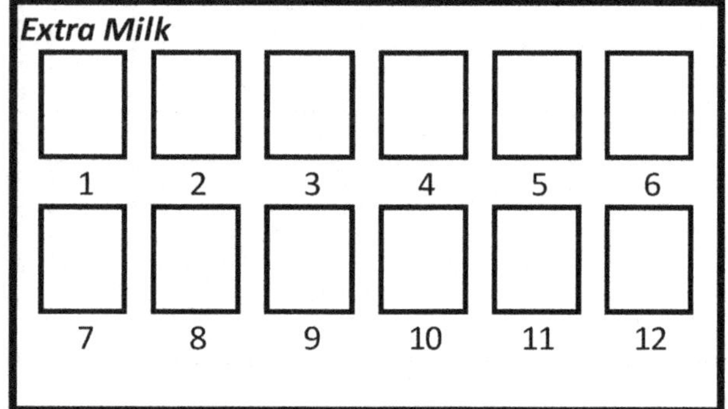

If pumping was needed, *how many milliliters* did you get from both breasts combined?

Pumped

1 2 3 4 5 6

7 8 9 10 11 12

How much *total* milk did you pump *today* ?

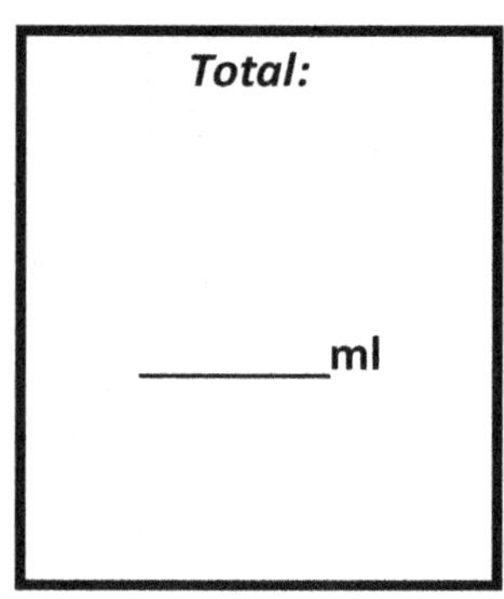

How many times did the baby poop today?

Poops

It is ok if you have more poops than boxes provided.

Goal of 4 or more today

Helpful tips for today

* Your baby should be back to birthweight. If not, meet with your IBCLC after seeing your pediatrician.

* Keep enjoying your baby!

Questions and Notes:

Baby's weight today:__________

Combination Journal

Phase Three- Maintining Your Full Milk Supply

DAY 14 of Age

What **did you feed your baby at this feeding?**

B-Breastfeeding PM- Pumped Milk IF- Infant Formula

If extra milk is needed, *how much* did the baby take in milliliters?

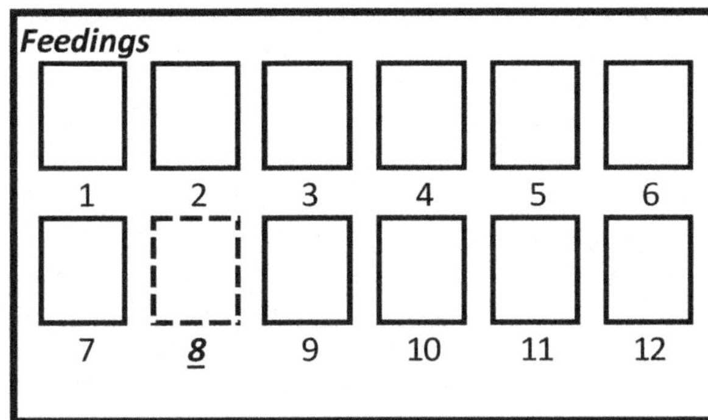

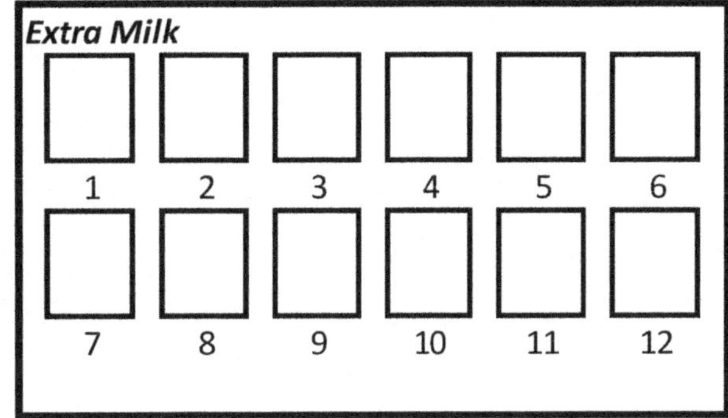

If pumping is needed, *how many milliliters* did you get from both breasts combined?

How much *total* milk did you pump *today* ?

Pumped

1 2 3 4 5 6

7 8 9 10 11 12

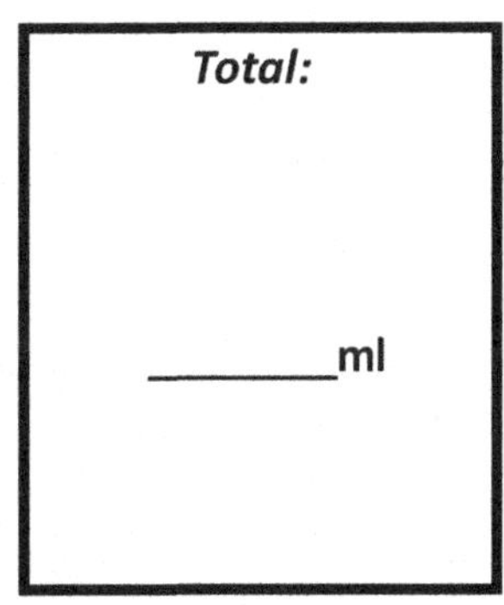

How many times did the baby poop today?

Poops

It is ok if you have more poops than boxes provided.

Goal of 4 or more today

Helpful tips for today

* Congratulations! Your toughest days are behind you.

*If your baby isn't gaining well yet or you sense something isn't right, contact your IBCLC for additional help.

Questions and Notes:

Baby's weight today:__________

Notes

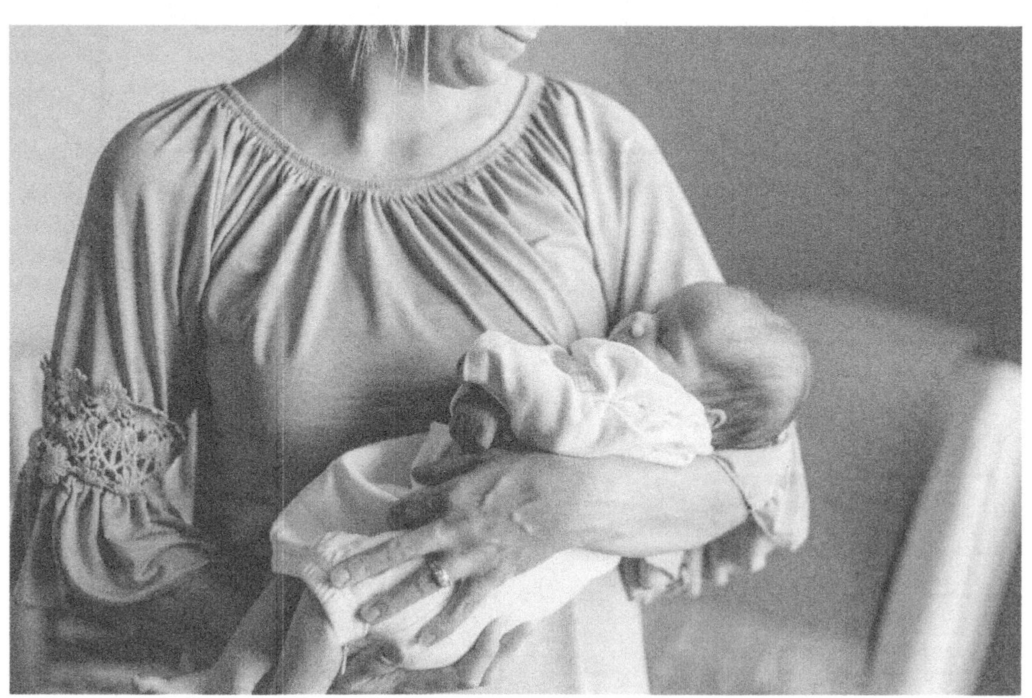

Notes

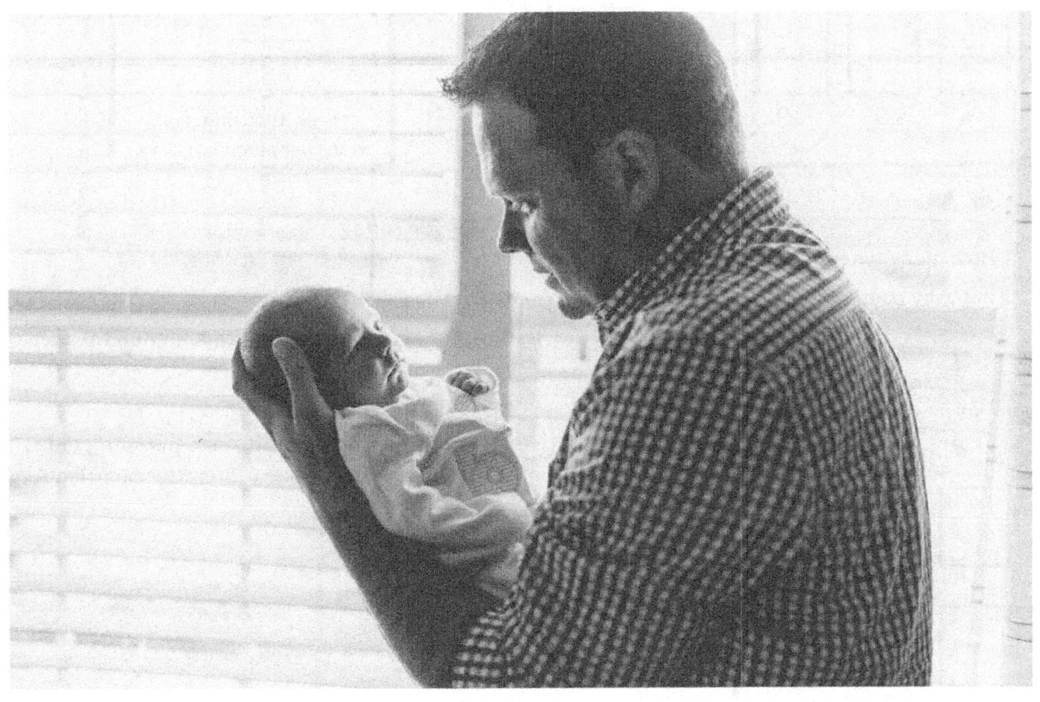

Exclusive Pumping Journal

Phase One- Initiating Your Milk Supply

DAY 1 of Age

How much *pumped breastmilk* did you feed the baby in milliliters?

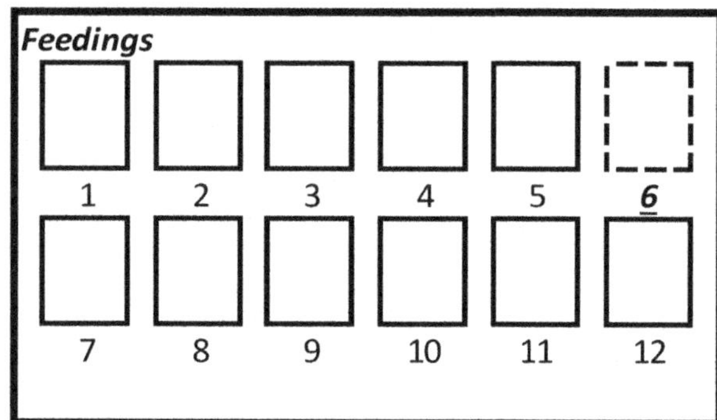

If *infant formula* was needed, how much did the baby take in milliliters?

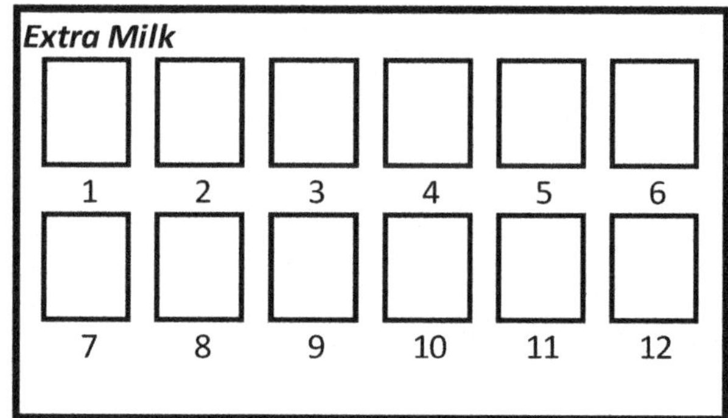

When you hand expressed and pumped, *how many milliliters* did you get from both breasts combined?

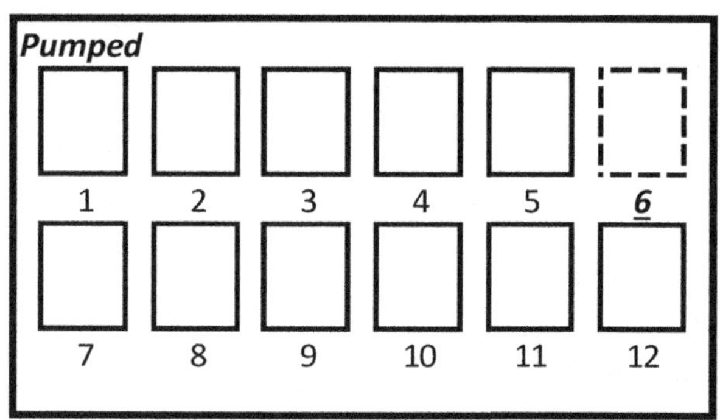

How much *total* milk did you pump *today*?

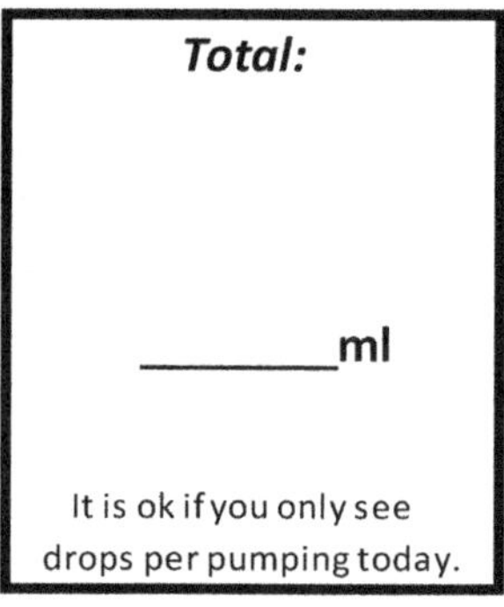

How many times did the baby poop today?

Poops

It is ok if you have more poops than boxes provided.

Goal of 1 or more today

Helpful tips for today

*Your baby may sleep between feedings today. If your baby is stable, lots of skin to skin contact is good for both of you, even if baby is not nursing.

*Use hand expression in addition to pumping today.
http://newborns.stanford.edu/Breastfeeding/HandExpression.html

Questions and Notes:

Baby's weight today:__________

Exclusive Pumping Journal

Phase One- Initiating Your Milk Supply

DAY 2 of Age

How much *pumped breastmilk* did you feed the baby in milliliters?

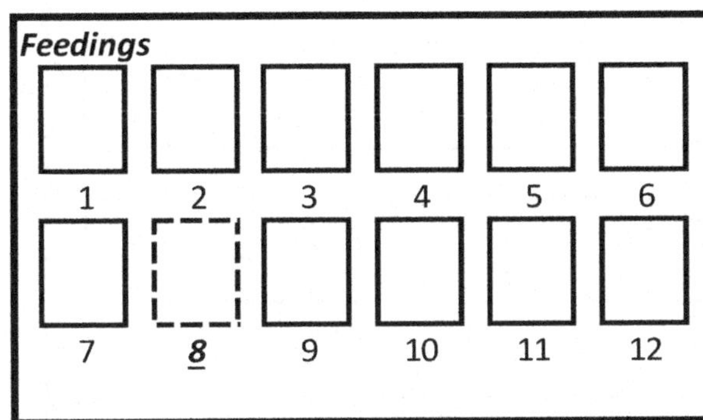

If *infant formula* was needed, how much did the baby take in milliliters?

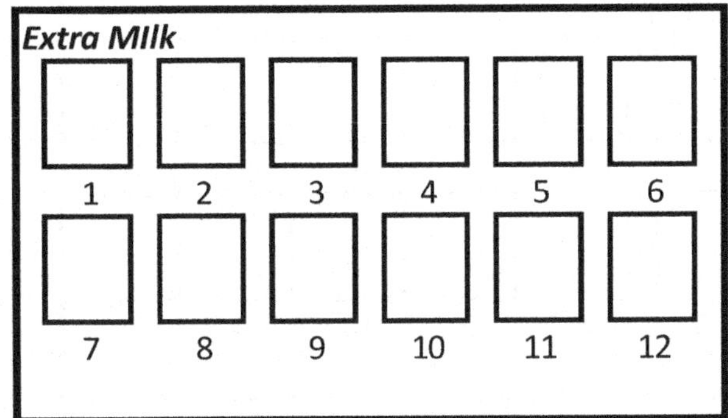

When you hand expressed and pumped, *how many* milliliters did you get from both breasts combined?

Pumped

1 2 3 4 5 6

7 8 9 10 11 12

How much *total* milk did you pump *today* ?

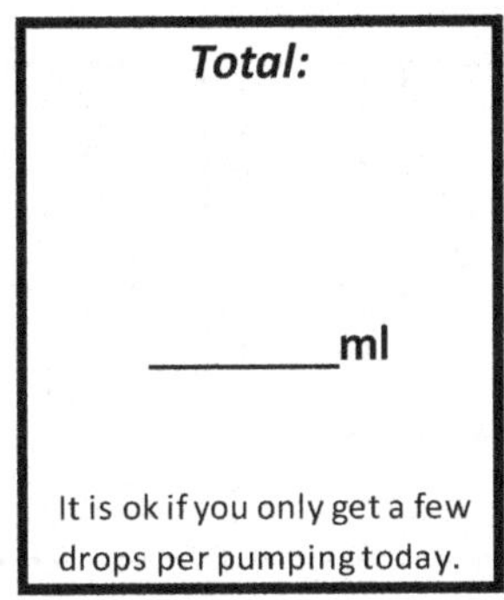

How many times did the baby poop today?

Poops

It is ok if you have more poops than boxes provided.

Goal of 2 or more today

Helpful tips for today

*Hand expression in addition to pumping today.

*If you need to sleep a longer stretch at night, you can pump every two hours during the day and still get 10 pumping sessions done. Someone else can feed the baby while you sleep. For example you could pump 5 am, 7 am, 9 am, 11 am, 1 pm, 3 pm, 5 pm, 7 pm, 9 pm, 11 pm, then sleep until 5 am.

Questions and Notes:

Baby's weight today:_________

Exclusive Pumping Journal

Phase One- Initiating Your Milk Supply

DAY 3 of Age

How much *pumped breastmilk* did you feed the baby in milliliters?

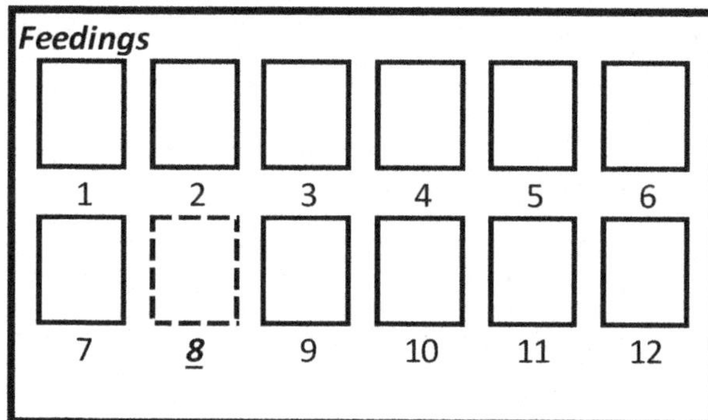

If *infant formula* was needed, how much did the baby take in milliliters?

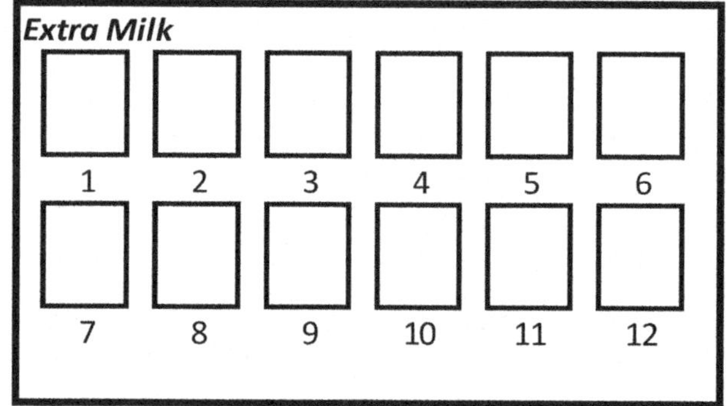

When you hand expressed and pumped, *how many* milliliters did you get from both breasts combined?

Pumped

1 2 3 4 5 6

7 8 9 ***10*** 11 12

How much *total* milk did you pump *today*?

How many times did the baby poop today?

Poops

It is ok if you have more poops than boxes provided.

Goal of 3 or more today

Helpful tips for today

*Your baby may be sleepy today and have some jaundice. See **Jaundice** page 31 and **Days and Nights** page 28.

*If your baby needs supplemental formula, request hypoallergenic. See **Bottles, Pacis, and Formula** page 45.

*Use breast massage while pumping.

* Hand expression before or after pumping might be helpful.

Questions and Notes:

Baby's weight today:____________

Exclusive Pumping Journal

Phase One- Initiating Your Milk Supply

DAY 4 of Age

How much *pumped breastmilk* did you feed the baby in milliliters?

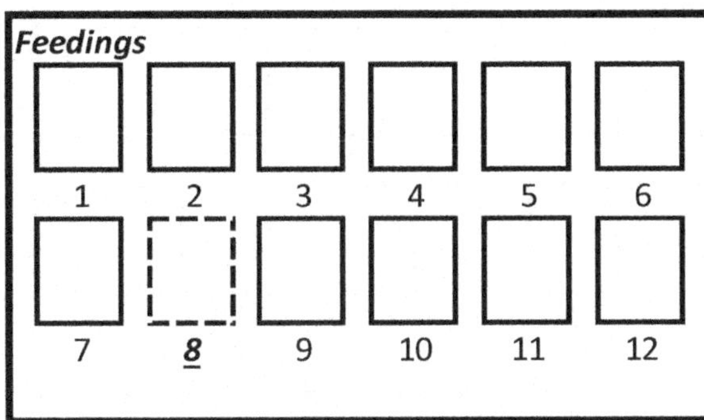

If *infant formula* was needed, how much did the baby take in milliliters?

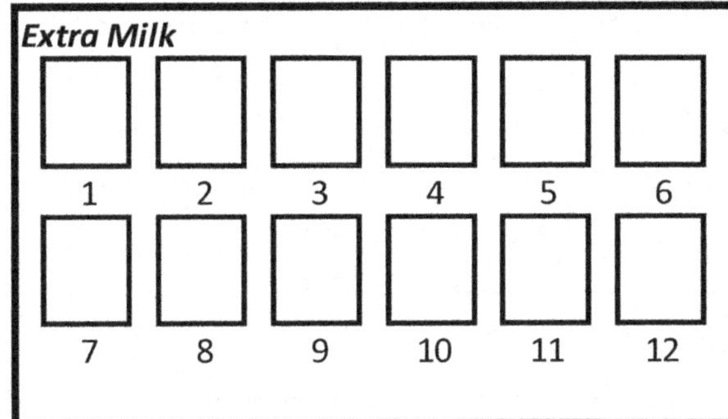

When you hand expressed and pumped, *how many* milliliters did you get from both breasts combined?

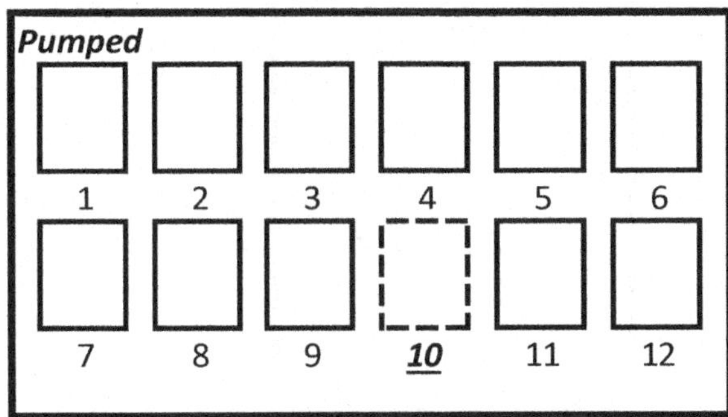

How much *total* milk did you pump *today*?

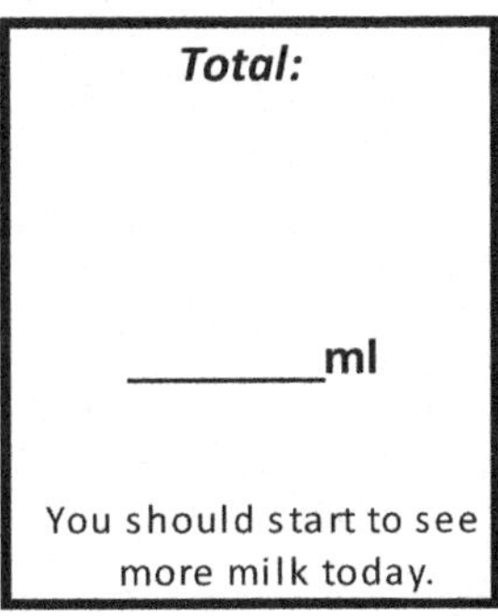

How many times did the baby poop today?

Poops

It is ok if you have more poops than boxes provided.

Goal of 4 or more today

Helpful tips for today

*Your baby may have some jaundice and be sleepy today. See **Jaudice** page 31 and **Days and Nights** page 28.

*If your breasts are uncomfortable or full, see **Breast Pain** page 26.

*Use breast massage while pumping.

Questions and Notes:

Baby's weight today:__________

Exclusive Pumping Journal

Phase Two- Growing Your Full Milk Supply

DAY 5 of Age

How much *pumped breastmilk* did you feed the baby in milliliters?

If *infant formula* was needed, how much did the baby take in milliliters?

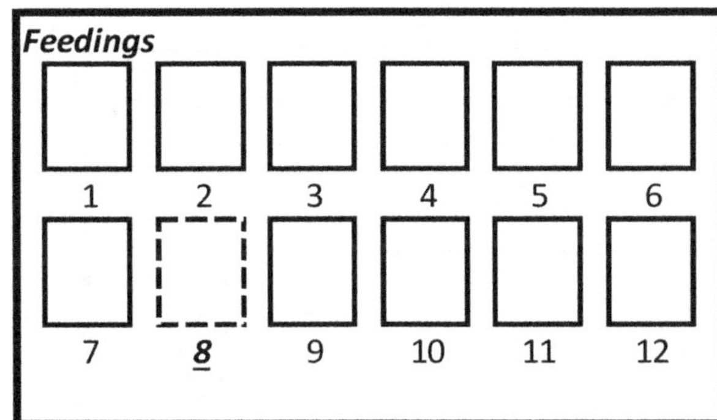

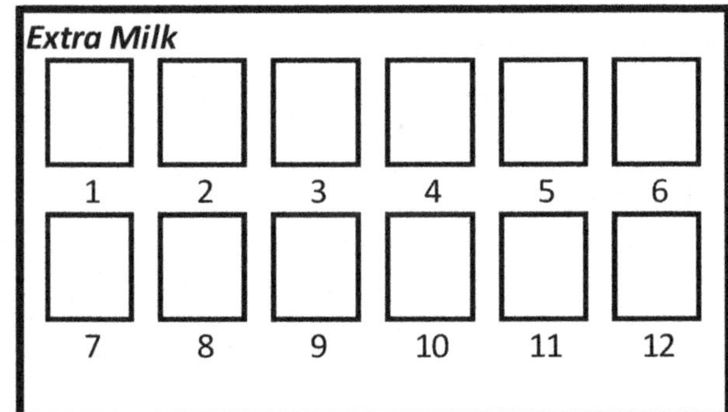

When you pumped, *how many milliliters* did you get from both breasts combined?

How much *total* milk did you pump *today*?

Pumped

1	2	3	4	5	6
7	8	9	***10***	11	12

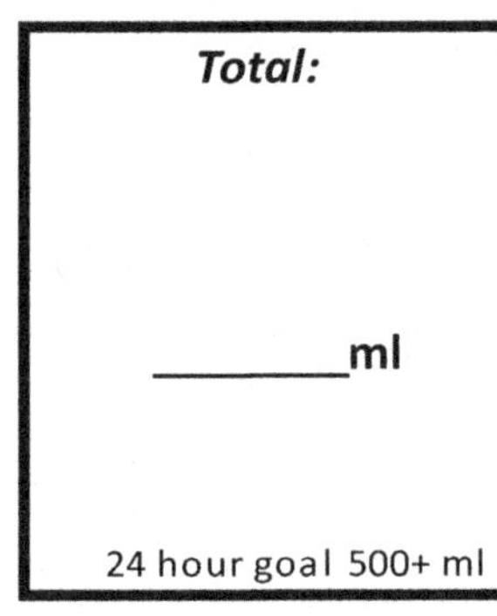

How many times did the baby poop today?

Poops

It is ok if you have more poops than boxes provided.

Goal of 4 or more today

Helpful tips for today

* Remember breast massage during each pumping.

* If you are not meeting your 24 hour goal, contact your IBCLC for tips to increase supply and continue pumping 10 times per day.

Questions and Notes:

Baby's weight today:__________

Exclusive Pumping Journal

Phase Two - Growing Your Full Milk Supply

DAY 6 of Age

How much *pumped breastmilk* did you feed the baby in milliliters?

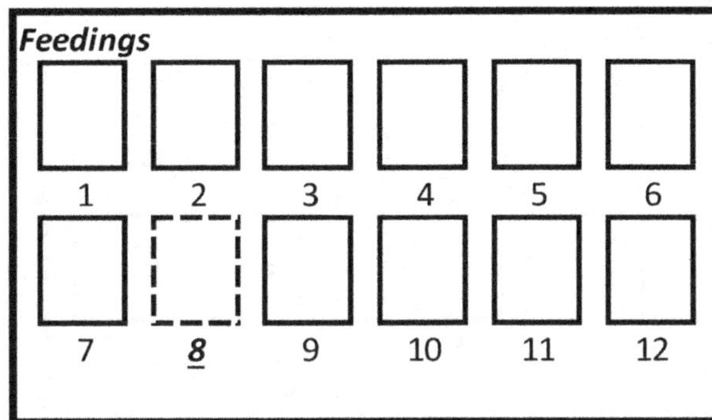

If *infant formula* was needed, how much did the baby take in milliliters?

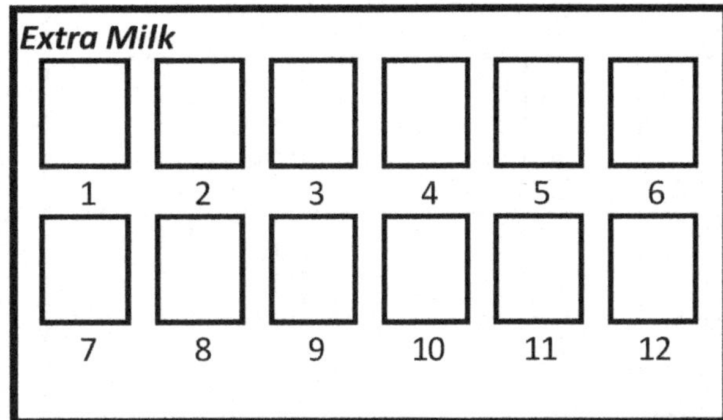

When you pumped, *how many milliliters* did you get from both breasts combined?

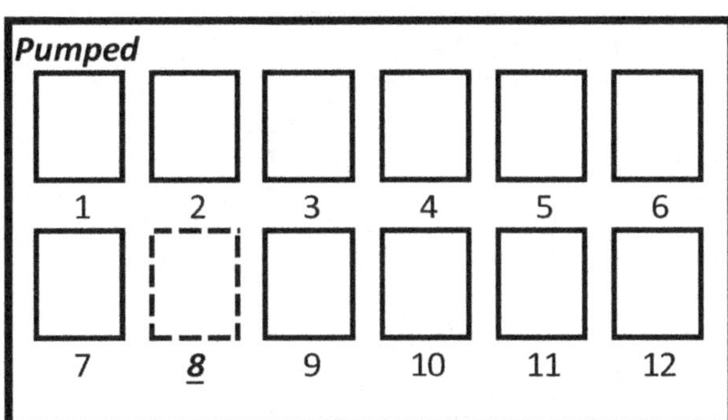

How much *total* milk did you pump *today*?

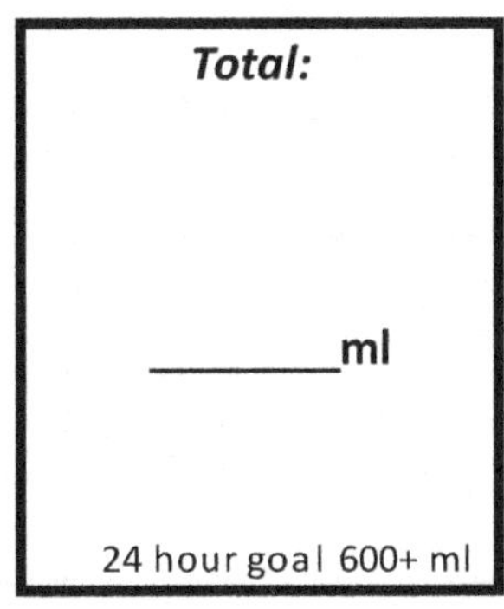

How many times did the baby poop today?

Poops

It is ok if you have more poops than boxes provided.

Goal of 4 or more today

Helpful tips for today

* During the day hold and feed your baby his bottle before pumping. Ask someone else to burp and diaper him while you are pumping.

* Ask for and accept help from your family and friends in these critical early days.

Questions and Notes:

Baby's weight today:__________

Exclusive Pumping Journal

Phase Two - Growing Your Full Milk Supply

DAY 7 of Age

How much *pumped breastmilk* did you feed the baby in milliliters?

If *infant formula* was needed, how much did the baby take in milliliters?

Feedings

1	2	3	4	5	6
7	***8***	9	10	11	12

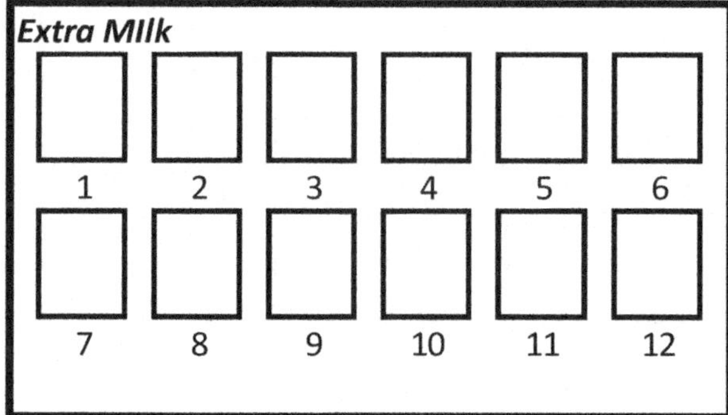

When you hand expressed and pumped, *how many* milliliters did you get from both breasts combined?

How much *total* milk did you pump *today*?

Pumped

1	2	3	4	5	6
7	***8***	9	10	11	12

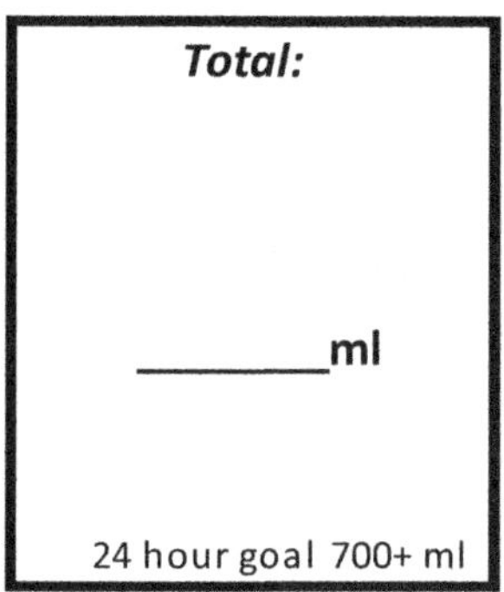

How many times did the baby poop today?

Poops

It is ok if you have more poops than boxes provided.

Goal of 4 or more today

Helpful tips for today

* Your baby might begin his first growth spurt today.

* If you are not meeting your 24 hour goal, contact your IBCLC for tips to increase supply and continue 10 pumpings per day.

Questions and Notes:

Baby's weight today:__________

Exclusive Pumping Journal

Phase Two - Growing Your Full Milk Supply

DAY 8 of Age

How much *pumped breastmilk* did you feed the baby in milliliters?

Feedings

1 2 3 4 5 6

7 8 9 10 11 12

If *infant formula* was needed, how much did the baby take in milliliters?

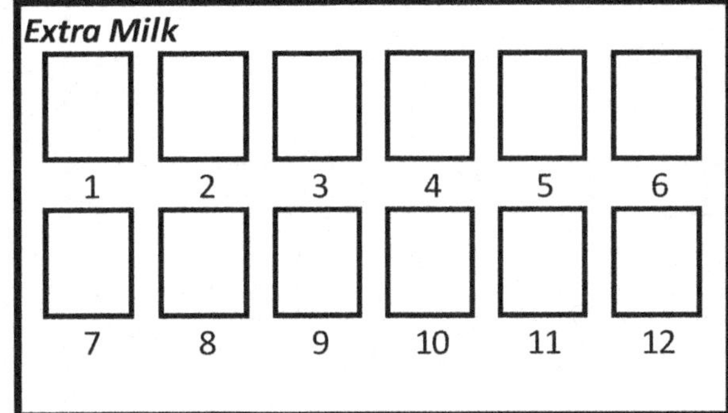

When you pumped, *how many milliliters* did you get from both breasts combined?

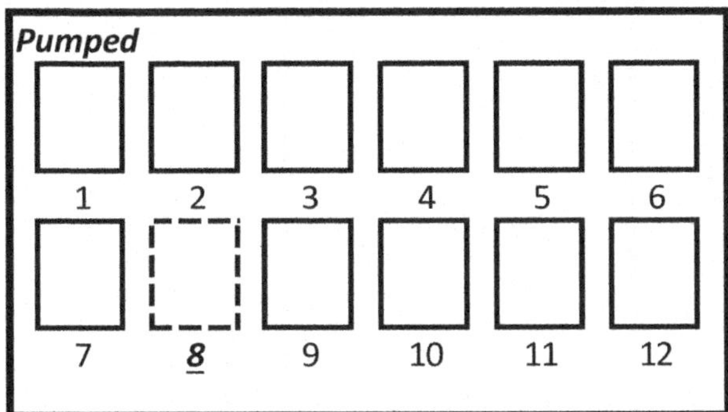

How much *total* milk did you pump *today*?

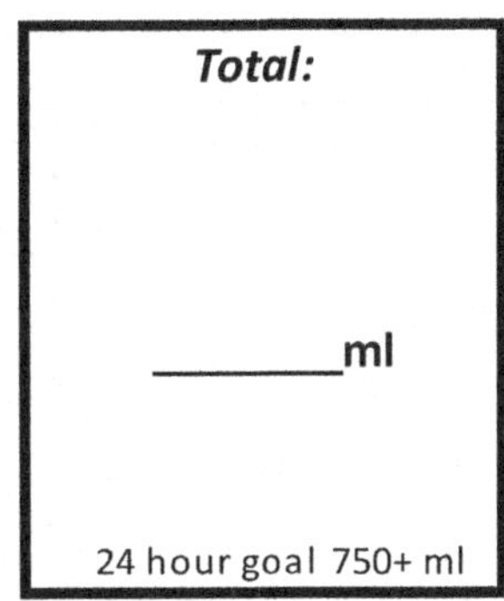

How many times did the baby poop today?

Poops

It is ok if you have more poops than boxes provided.

Goal of 4 or more today

Helpful tips for today

* Its is ok if your baby eats more often and takes more volume today.

* Your baby might be sleeping a lot. Babies grow during their deep sleep.

Questions and Notes:

Baby's weight today:__________

Exclusive Pumping Journal

Phase Two- Growing Your Full Milk Supply

DAY 9 of Age

How much *pumped breastmilk* did you feed the baby in milliliters?

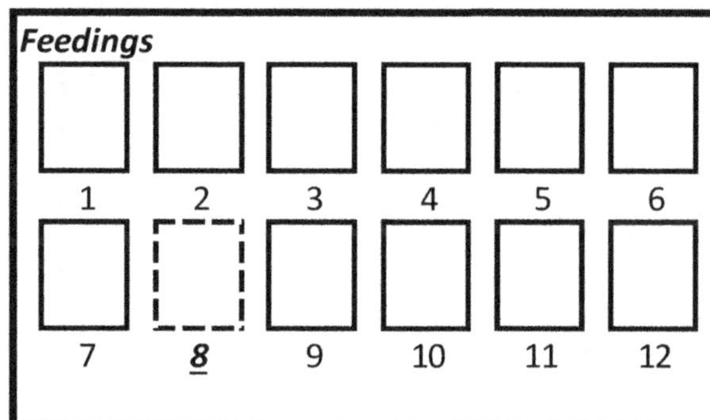

If *infant formula* was needed, how much did the baby take in milliliters?

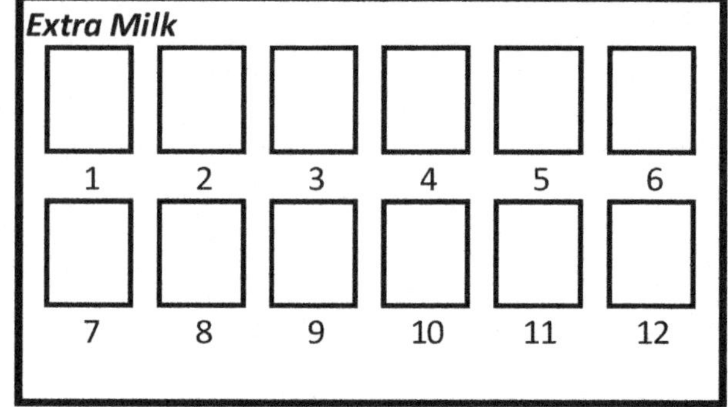

When you pumped, *how many milliliters* did you get from both breasts combined?

Pumped

1 2 3 4 5 6

7 ***8*** 9 10 11 12

How much *total* milk did you pump *today* ?

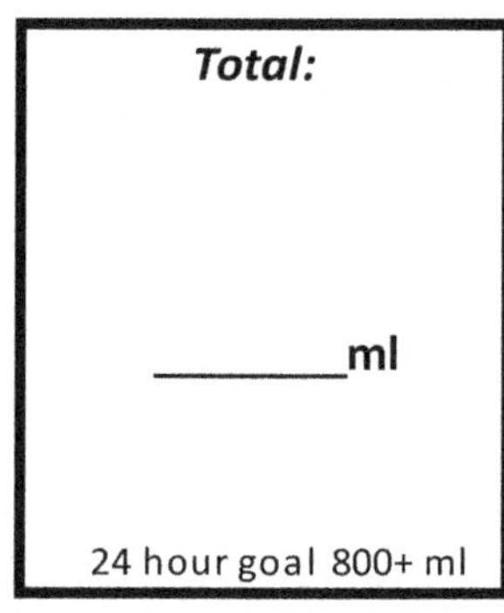

How many times did the baby poop today?

Poops

It is ok if you have more poops than boxes provided.

Goal of 4 or more today

Helpful tips for today

*Growth spurt continues today.

*Continue protecting sleep for both you and your baby.

Questions and Notes:

Baby's weight today:__________

Exclusive Pumping Journal

Phase Three - Maintaining Your Full Milk Supply

DAY 10 of Age

How much *pumped breastmilk* did you feed the baby in milliliters?

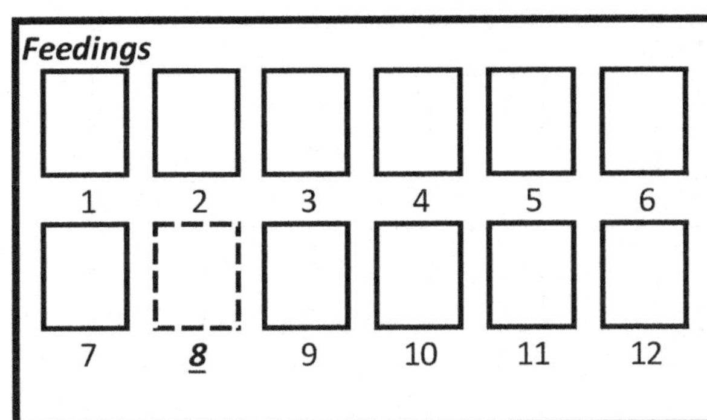

If *infant formula* was needed, how much did the baby take in milliliters?

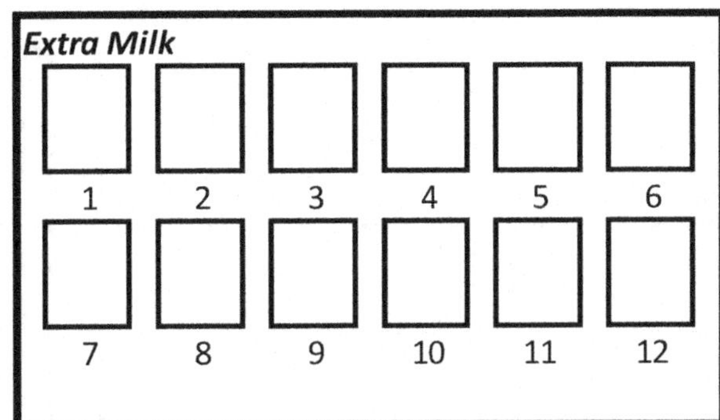

When you pumped, *how many milliliters* did you get from both breasts combined?

Pumped

1 2 3 4 5 6

7 8 9 10 11 12

How much *total* milk did you pump *today*?

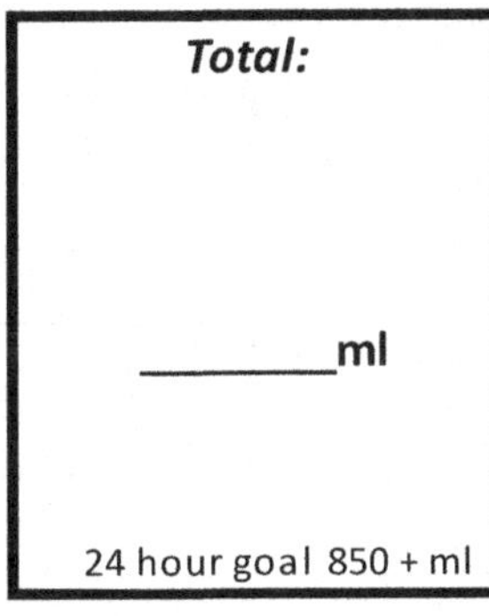

How many times did the baby poop today?

Poops

It is ok if you have more poops than boxes provided.

Goal of 4 or more today

Helpful tips for today

*If your 24 hour milk production is below 750 ml, contact your IBCLC for help.

* Keep enjoying your baby!

Questions and Notes:

Baby's weight today:__________

Exclusive Pumping Journal

Phase Three - Maintaining Your Full Milk Supply

DAY 11 of Age

How much *pumped breastmilk* did you feed the baby in milliliters?

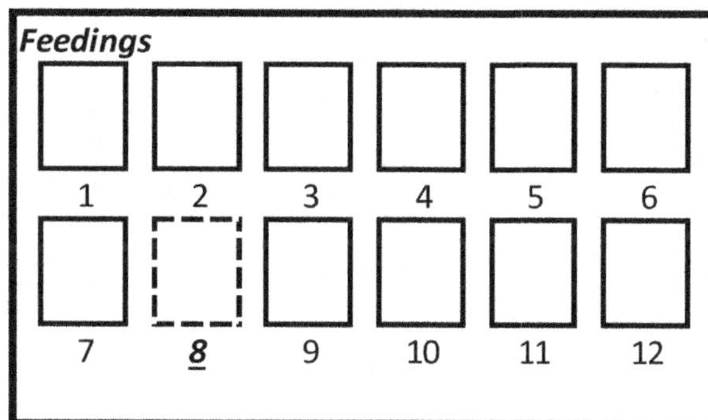

If *infant formula* was needed, how much did the baby take in milliliters?

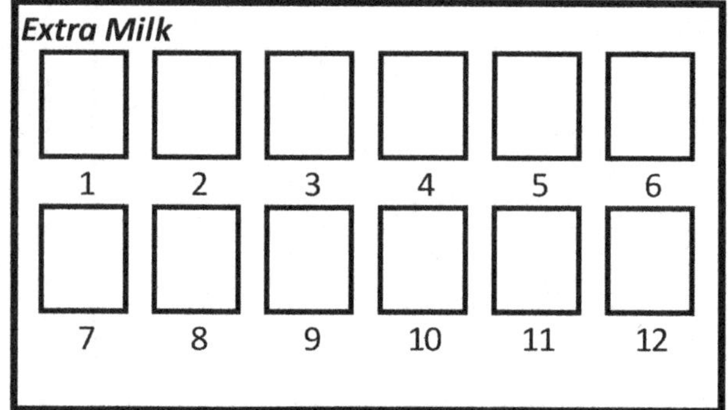

When you pumped, *how many milliliters* did you get from both breasts combined?

Pumped

1	2	3	4	5	6
7	8	9	10	11	12

How much *total* milk did you pump *today*?

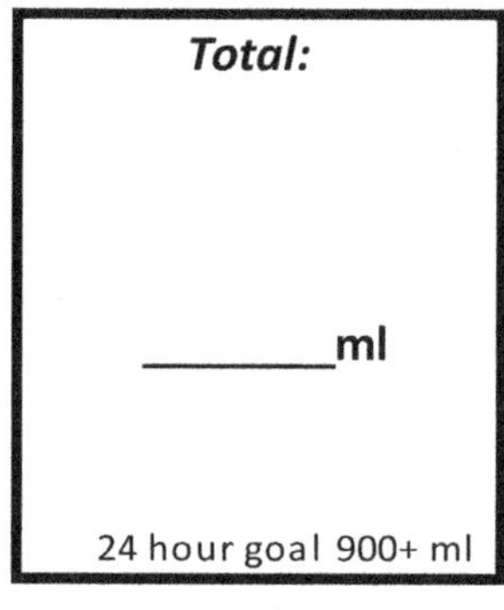

How many times did the baby poop today?

Poops

It is ok if you have more poops than boxes provided.

Goal of 4 or more today

Helpful tips for today

* As long as your 24 hour total is greater than 750 ml, you are on track to establish a full supply.

*Your baby may settle into a 2-3 hour daytime and 3-4 hour nightime feeding rhythm. You can go as long as 4 hours at night between pumpings as long as you are meeting your 24 hour goal.

Questions and Notes:

Baby's weight today:__________

Exclusive Pumping Journal

Phase Three - Maintaining Your Full Milk Supply

DAY 12 of Age

How much *pumped breastmilk* did you feed the baby in milliliters?

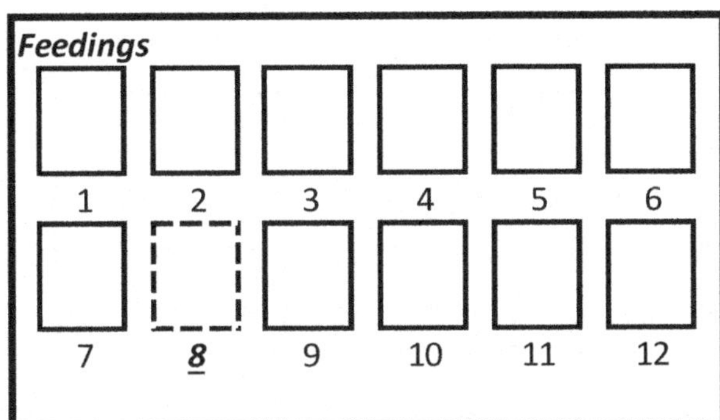

If *infant formula* was needed, how much did the baby take in milliliters?

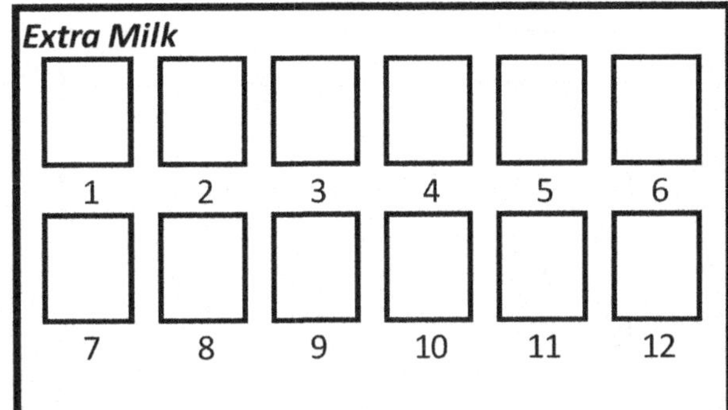

When you pumped, *how many milliliters* did you get from both breasts combined?

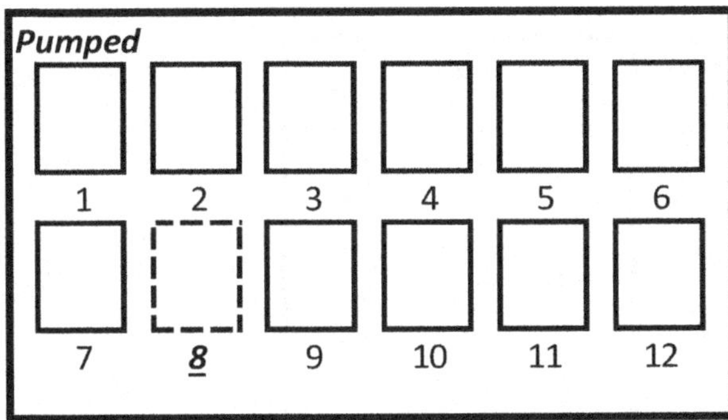

How much *total* milk did you pump *today*?

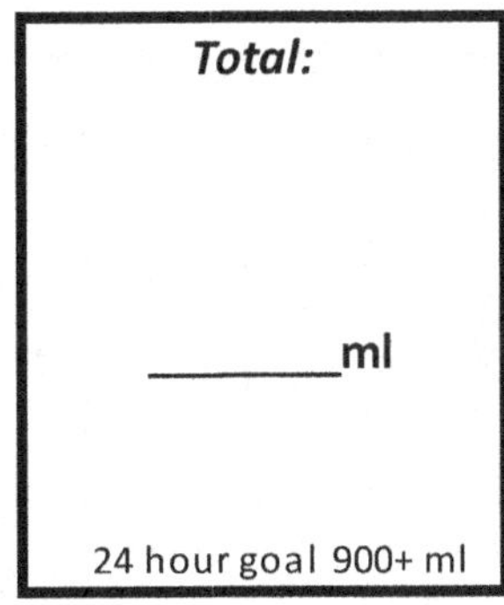

How many times did the baby poop today?

Poops

It is ok if you have more poops than boxes provided.

☐ ☐ ☐ ☐

☐ ☐ ☐ ☐

Goal of 4 or more today

Helpful tips for today

* If your 24 hour total is less than 750 ml, contact your IBCLC for tips to increase your milk production.

* Keep protecting your rest.

* If your 24 hour total is more than 1000ml, talk to your IBCLC about pumping less minutes per pumping.

Questions and Notes:

Baby's weight today:__________

Exclusive Pumping Journal

Phase Three - Maintaining Your Full Milk Supply

DAY 13 of Age

How much *pumped breastmilk* did you feed the baby in milliliters?

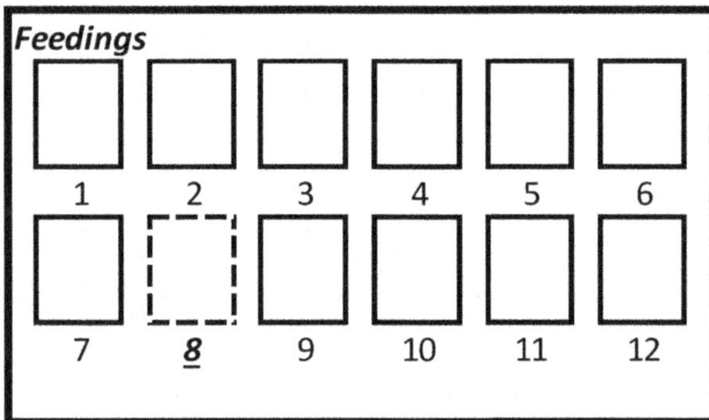

If *infant formula* was needed, how much did the baby take in milliliters?

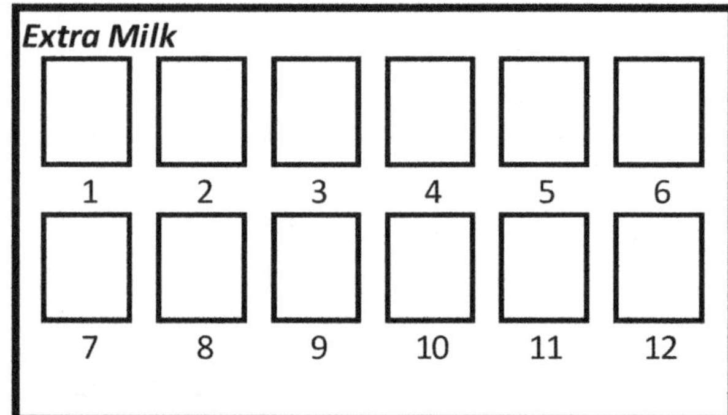

When you pumped, *how many milliliters* did you get from both breasts combined?

Pumped

1 2 3 4 5 6

7 8 9 10 11 12

How much *total* milk did you pump *today*?

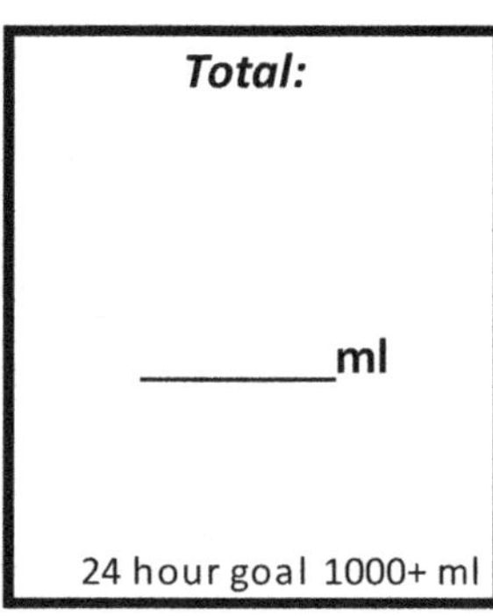

How many times did the baby poop today?

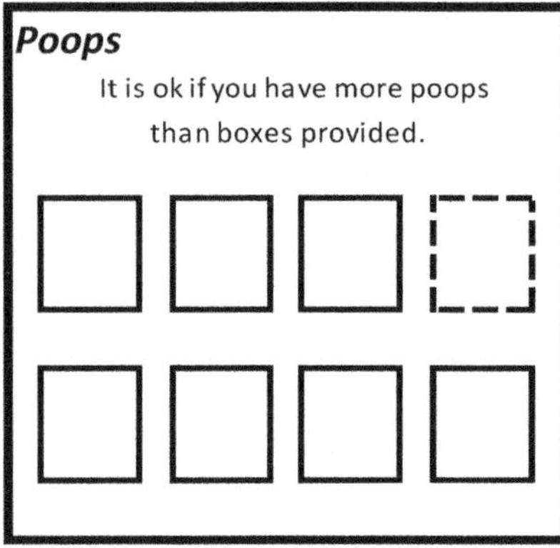

Goal of 4 or more today

Helpful tips for today

* If your 24 hour total is less than 750 ml, contact your IBCLC for additional help.

* If you and your baby are ready to transition back to the breast, **See Going Back to the Breast** page 51.

Questions and Notes:

Baby's weight today:__________

Exclusive Pumping Journal

Phase Three - Maintaining Your Full Milk Supply

DAY 14 of Age

How much *pumped breastmilk* did you feed the baby in milliliters?

If *infant formula* was needed, how much did the baby take in milliliters?

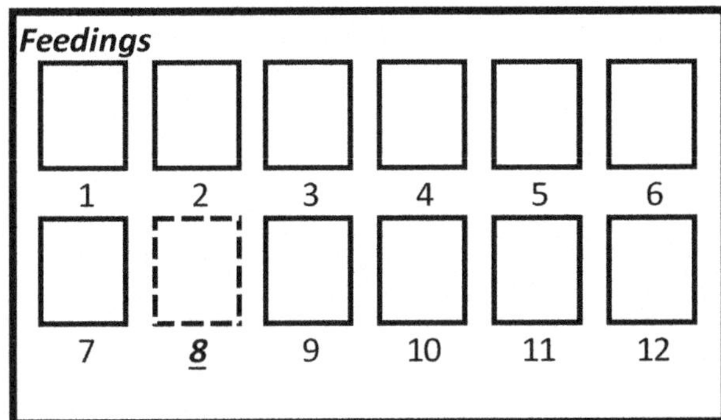

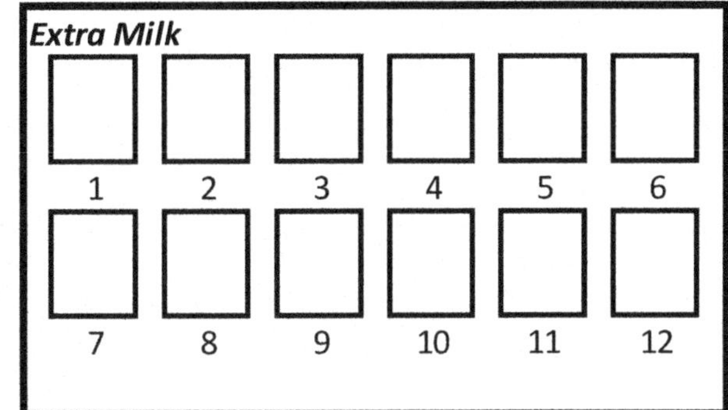

When you pumped, *how many milliliters* did you get from both breasts combined?

How much *total* milk did you pump *today* ?

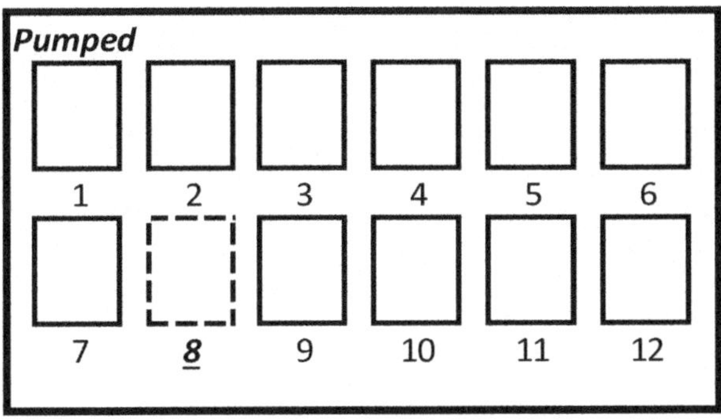

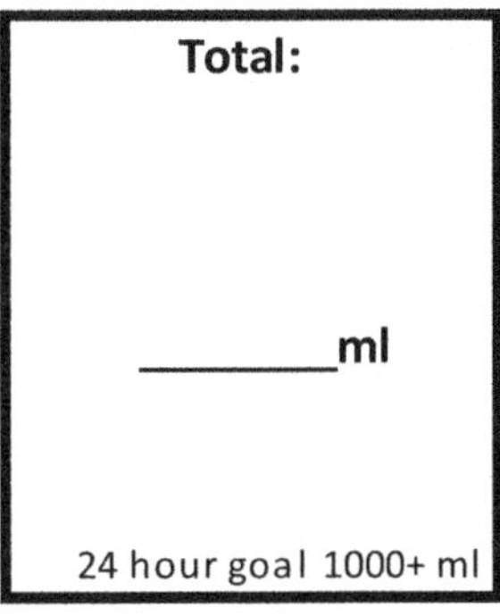

How many times did the baby poop today?

Poops

It is ok if you have more poops than boxes provided.

Goal of 4 or more today

Helpful tips for today

*Your baby should be back to birthweight today. If not, make an appointment to meet with your IBCLC after seeing your pediatrican.

* If you and your baby are ready to begin the transition back to the breast, see **Going Back to the Breast** page 51.

Questions and Notes:

Baby's weight today:__________

Made in the USA
Middletown, DE
27 December 2018